Christianity for Skeptics

Christianity for Skeptics

An Understandable Examination of Christian Belief

STEVE KUMAR

Illustrations by Neil Dishington

HENDRICKSON
PUBLISHERS

To Joy
for
her unfailing love

Christianity for Skeptics

Hendrickson Publishers, Inc.
P. O. Box 3473,
Peabody, Massachusetts 01961-3473

Copyright © 2000 John Hunt Publishing Ltd.
Text copyright © 1996 Steve Kumar
Illustrations copyright © 2000 Neil Dishington

ISBN 1-56563-346-6

First published 1987
Reissued under the title *Christianity for Skeptics* in 2000

Reprinted in 2001

Designed and produced by Tony Cantale Graphics

Write to:
John Hunt Publishing Ltd, 46A West Street,
Alresford, Hampshire SO24 9AU, UK.

Printed in Italy

CONTENTS

FOREWORD

We are living in an age in which ideologies rule and rule often without much evidence for their truth. The world is veering towards humanism. Neo-Darwinism, developed from the theories put forward by Darwin some 140 years ago fits with this trend, for it too believes that natural law, the laws of matter and the space-time continuum are the be all and end all of reality. Thus any ideologies involving metaphysics and God are retrograde—for neither God nor metaphysics really exist. That is the view.

Yet at the same time as these "scientifically" based trends to humanism and atheism are developing, the innate religious nature of man is asserting itself with a vengeance. Thus we have the resurgence of occultism, eastern cults and religions old and new (Islam and New Age as examples) while the ideology of materialism political as well as "religious" grows up all around us at the same time. Thus anti-polar and antithetical ideologies grow and flourish in most modern societies. The skeptics are often to be found in the academic scientific circles while the occult and metaphysical ideologies are widespread among the lay people, philosophers and the theologians too.

As a result of these antithetical developments, confusion amongst students and thinkers has grown enormously in recent years. For they in the colleges, universities and media are confronted with both trends—and few are the clear thinkers who are in a position to help them focus their thought. If these tendencies go on unchecked we shall find ourselves in the position which C. S. Lewis so beautifully described, namely that of the pure materialist believing in ghosts and spirits—the materialistic occult magician!

It is for this reason that I recommend Dr. Steve Kumar's book. It gives a clear and balanced view on the subjects above mentioned and will help, if well digested, to clear away some of the mists of simultaneous antitheses which so easily befog the thoughtful young academics of today.

Professor A. E. Wilder-Smith, B.Sc., Ph.D., Dr.es.Sc., Dr.Sc., F.R.S.C.(London), former Professor of Pharmacology at the Medical Center, University of Illinois.

CHAPTER 1

"The greatest question
of our time is not communism vs.
individualism, nor Europe vs. America,
nor even the East vs. the West; it is
whether men can bear to live
without God."
WILL DURANT

"The mathematical precision of
the universe reveals the mathematical
mind of God."
ALBERT EINSTEIN

"I shall always be convinced
that a watch proves a watch-maker,
and that a universe proves a God."
VOLTAIRE

DOES GOD EXIST?

Is it reasonable to believe in God? Can God's existence be logically proven without appealing to religious experience or a leap of faith? Is God merely a psychological projection, a primitive myth? How could anyone be sure there is a God? What evidence supports God's existence?

Our secular culture may dismiss God as irrelevant to our existence and give the seductive impression that God is on a long vacation. This popular myth may provide some humans with a sense of freedom and autonomy, but it has not delivered us from boredom, anxiety, suicide, stress, drugs, crime, addiction to entertainment, and other neuroses.[1] After diagnosing the human predicament, psychiatrist Victor Frankl observes, **"More people today have the means to live, but no meaning to live for."**[2] According to Erich Fromm, one of the leading specialists in human behavior, the majority of those who visit psychiatrists suffer from **"an inner deadness. They live in the midst of plenty and are joyless."**[3]

In the light of our social and spiritual crisis it is not beyond reason to propose that the missing element in our recipe for existence is the reality of God.[4] History has repeatedly confirmed the tragic truth that when people ignore the Transcendent they descend into the abyss of nihilism. Where God is abandoned, human life becomes, in the words of Thomas Hubb, **"nasty, brutish and short."** There is no song of hope but only the cry of despair.[5]

THE RELEVANCE OF GOD

The reality of God's existence has serious consequences to human existence. No other issue touches our lives as does this subject. It has a profound philosophical implication on all matters of reality. "**The greatest question of our time,**" notes Will Durant, "**is whether men can bear to live without God.**"[6] Chicago philosopher and director of the Institute for Philosophical Research, Mortimer Adler, agrees, "**More consequences for thought and action follow the affirmation or denial of God than from answering any other basic question.**"[7]

It is vital to reflect on the relevance of God before we demonstrate the reality of God. The existence of God plays a significant role in our lives. Superficially many may not acknowledge this reality, but upon deeper reflection, the relevance of God is inescapable.

Some time ago a New York police officer observed a man standing on a bridge, apparently thinking of committing suicide. The policeman approached him and said, "Let me make a deal with you. Give me ten minutes to tell you why I think life is worth living, then you take ten minutes and tell me why you think life is not worth living. If I am unable to convince you, I will let you jump." According to the story, after twenty minutes they joined hands and both jumped off the bridge.

The story poses serious questions. Is life really worth living? If there is no God, what is the reason for our being? What is the logical ground for our values, morality, rationality, dignity, and personality? If there is no God, we are, in the words of philosopher William James, like dogs in a library observing the volumes but unable to read the print. Are we just an accidental by-product of matter evolved mindlessly on an infinitesimal speck of dust called Planet Earth? How could we find meaning in a meaningless universe? Reason in an irrational world? Value in a material universe and purpose in a random existence? If there is no God, should we not conclude with Shakespeare that life "**is a tale told by an idiot, full of sound and fury, signifying nothing**"? How could we possibly escape the nihilism of Friedrich Nietzsche, the meaninglessness of Jean-Paul Sartre, the despair of Bertrand Russell, the nothingness of Martin Heidegger, or the suicide of Albert Camus? The absence of God in reality is the absence of goodness, truth, value, meaning, reason, life, and joy. Many of our brilliant minds have understood only too well the truth that the rejection of God logically implies the rejection of all reality that is fundamental to God.[8]

Although the subject of God may appear to be simple on the surface, it is an extremely profound matter. God is not a secondary issue but an ultimate factor. The very nature of God demands an approach that transcends the normal and the contingent. One should not attempt to prove God the way we try to prove apples and atoms. The reality of God is in a category that is radically trans-natural – that which is beyond and above nature. God is transcendent.[9] One must not commit the categorical mistake of equating God with the phenomena which he has made.[10]

If God is the cause of the universe, he must be beyond and greater than the physical dimension. Therefore we may discover the effects or evidence of God in the universe but not necessarily observe the essence of God within the universe, for the profound reason that he transcends the categories of space, time, and matter. The skeptic who says, "Show me your God!" and demands a scientific proof, is extremely simplistic.

The story of the man who went fishing illustrates an important truth. Every time he caught a big fish he kept throwing it back into the lake, and each time he caught a small one, he kept it. A mystified bystander, observing his peculiar process of selection, asked him what on earth he was doing. With a smile the man replied, "I only have an eight inch frying pan and so the larger fish won't fit." The trouble is, many a skeptic rejects God because God won't fit into their naturalistic philosophical frying pan. The truth is, there are realities which go beyond our limited paradigm, but to reject them because they do not fit our limited scientific category is to become a poor metaphysical fisherman. The trouble with our naturalistic metaphysical frying pan is that it is not big enough to include all of reality.[11]

The question of God's existence is a perennial issue which presses upon all of us and demands a rational response. To go through life without examining ultimate questions is to miss the central point of human existence. The meaning of life is to find the meaning for life, and the purpose of existence is to discover the purpose worth living for. A sensible existence is possible only when we try to make sense of our lives and the universe. As Socrates so wisely proposed, "The unexamined life is not worth living."[12] Reflection can lead us to resolution. Philosopher Elton Trueblood, in addressing this issue, suggests, "If we refuse to discuss the existence of God we are simply avoiding the central issue, which is the issue of delusion."[13] Even the Oxford atheistic philosopher J. L. Mackie agrees that the issue of God's existence is worth reflection. He insists, "The question whether there is or is not a god can and should be rewarding, in that it can yield definite results."[14] In the final analysis, as Thomistic philosopher Edward Sillem affirms, "The conclusion we reach in our reflection on this question has the most momentous consequences in the orientation of our thinking and of our daily living."[15] If there is a God, knowing him will be the ultimate key to our existence. This truth would be the greatest truth for mankind. Unlike any other questions, the question of God has cosmic significance, for it touches every realm of our existence and provides the basic reason for our being.

Since the concept of God's existence is the greatest issue confronting humanity, it deserves our most thoughtful attention. Evangelical philosopher C. Stephen Evans affirms, "Belief in God is genuinely coherent with all we know about ourselves and our universe. It contradicts no known facts and it makes sense of many things that would otherwise be inexplicable."[16]

Time magazine, in an interesting article, "Modernizing the Case for God," reports, "In a quiet revolution in thought and argument that hardly anyone could have foreseen only two decades ago, God is making a comeback." A generation ago there were few intellectuals in academic circles providing logical arguments for the existence of God, but today the situation has altered. As *Time* suggests, "Now it is more respectable among philosophers than it has been for a generation to talk about the possibility of God's existence."[17]

Great thinkers who affirm the existence of God have left a legacy of arguments for us to reflect upon. We will examine several of them. These arguments have been reinforced by recent developments in contemporary logic, philosophical arguments, and a number of scientific data. They are valuable in supporting our confidence in the reality of God.[18]

1. CONCLUSIVE COSMOLOGICAL EVIDENCE

In the opinion of many Christian philosophers, one of the most forceful arguments for the existence of God is the cosmic evidence.[19] The existence of the universe is an undeniable reality. The fact of existence is indeed a mystery which staggers the mind. Sophists may deny the reality of the universe, but such an attempt is futile, for the Sophist must exist in order to deny it, therefore it is self-refuting. A good case in point is the example of a student at New York University who troubled his professor with a contradictory question, "Sir, how do I know that I exist?" The professor paused for a while, lowered his glasses, gazed at the student and demanded, "And whom shall I say is asking?" The notion that existence is an illusion is logically incoherent and factually meaningless.

The most profound philosophical question that has caused many debates and much discussion among philosophers is, "Why is there something, rather than nothing?" The reality of the universe demands a verdict. There is hardly a philosopher worth a grain of salt who has not struggled over this question. Every thinking person at some point confronts the problem. Philosopher John Hick writes:

■ **When we try to think about this infinitely fascinating universe in which we live we find that we are faced in the end with the mystery of existence, of why there is a universe at all.**[20]

Philosopher and theologian H. D. Lewis from London University notes, "The question 'Why is there something rather than nothing?' is regarded even by some skeptical philosophers as a significant one."[21] This question caused considerable philosophical speculation for the German philosopher Gottfried Wilhelm Leibniz, who finally came to the conclusion that, "The first question which should rightly be asked is: Why is there something rather than nothing?"[22] Indeed, the fact is that we are existing rather than that we are not. Existential theologian Paul Tillich admits that "the riddle of all riddles" is the mystery that there is anything at all.[23] The question of Being, as Martin Heidegger pointed out, is the most significant of all questions and deserves every energy of our intellectual effort.

The writings of great minds such as Augustine, Thomas Aquinas, Descartes, Hegel, Dostoyevsky, Martin Heidegger, Jean-Paul Sartre, Ludwig Wittgenstein, C. S. Lewis, and others, indicate that the question of existence is worthy of serious reflection. Ludwig Wittgenstein, after reflecting on the mystery of existence, makes this significant point, "It is not how things are in the world that is mystical, but *that* it exists." This is an important observation in the light of his philosophical stature. His conclusion is even more startling, "The solution of the riddle of life in space and time lies *outside* space and time."[24] According to Wittgenstein, the answer to the question, "Why is there something rather than nothing?" lies not in the something, but beyond the something. In this sense Wittgenstein affirms that the fact of existence demands a ground for its existence, and the contingency of existence requires a non-contingent Being who is the cause of all contingency.

Philosopher David H. Freeman, in his important work, *A Philosophical*

Study of Religion, correctly observes, "The issue is whether the world is explicable solely in terms of itself, i.e. is the world itself ultimate, or is there a being other than the world to which the world is related?"[25] John Warwick Montgomery, the brilliant American apologist, argues along the same line, "Nothing in this world is able to explain its own existence; thus, there must be a God in order to explain the world in which we find ourselves."[26] Therefore, the most rational option for the thinking mind in reference to the universe is the reality of God. Without God the universe makes no sense.

Edward Sillem insists, "Man cannot find the ultimate explanation of his own being anywhere but in God Himself."[27] In the same vein, philosopher Fredrick Copleston asserts, "What we call the world is intrinsically unintelligible, apart from the existence of God."[28] It is no wonder that Voltaire echoed the obvious maxim, "If God did not exist it would be necessary to invent him." Speaking about the universe, Colin Brown, the British theologian, writes, "Are we to regard it as the product of pure chance, and believe that everything happens at random without rhyme or reason?"[29] No! This would be mental suicide. Even a radical skeptic such as David Hume admitted the force of this argument when he wrote, "I never asserted so absurd a proposition as that anything might arise without a cause."[30]

The weight of the cosmological argument is further strengthened by the confirmation of the majority of scientists today. Dr. Robert Gange, a research scientist, in his excellent book, *Origins and Destiny*, provides ample scientific evidence for the beginning of the universe. In the past scientists believed that the First Law of Thermodynamics led to a "steady state" theory of the universe: that the universe and everything in it has existed in one form or other forever. However, Dr. Gange notes, "Today, there's a problem with this idea *because the beginning of the universe has actually been measured. Although the measurement is indirect, it nonetheless teaches that there actually was a beginning!*"[31] He illustrates the measurement by comparing it to someone's firing a shotgun in another room. A minute later, we could walk into the room and observe the smoke still drifting from the end of the barrel. In a similar fashion, the "smoke" from the creation (Big Bang) is currently moving throughout the universe. This smoke, known as the background radiation of the universe, was measured by two leading scientists who later received the Nobel prize. This discovery demonstrates that the universe had a beginning. Dr. Gange concludes:

> ■ **Thus, the older idea of an eternally existing world is now known to have a problem. These measurements of what scientists call the background radiation that fills the universe tell us that the world is not eternal, but that it actually had a beginning.**[32]

Robert Jastrow, director of the NASA's Goddard Institute for Space Studies and author of many important studies in astronomy, comes to a similar conclusion. Writing in the *New York Times* Jastrow poses the question, "Have astronomers found God?" and suggests that they have, or are very close to it. Dr. Jastrow, who claims to be an agnostic, argues that the evidence from astronomy demonstrates that the universe had a beginning at a certain moment in time. He declares, "Now we see how the astronomical evidence leads to a biblical view of the origin of the world." He notes, "The details differ, but the essential elements in the astronomical and biblical accounts of Genesis are the same: the chain of events leading to man commenced suddenly and sharply at a definite moment in time, in a flash of light and energy." His brilliant conclusion is worth reflection:

> ■ **For the scientist who has lived by his faith in the power of reason, the story ends like a bad dream. He has scaled the mountains of ignorance; he is about to conquer the highest peak; as he pulls himself over the final rock, he is greeted by a band of theologians who have been sitting there for centuries.**[33]

The apostle Paul speaking to the Greek philosophers of his day argued that the existence of the universe provided good and sufficient reason to trust in the existence of God:

> ■ **The God who made the world and everything in it is the Lord of heaven and earth and does not live in temples built by hands. And he is not served by human**

hands, as if he needed anything, because he himself gives all men life and breath and everything else. "For in him we live and move and have our being" (Acts 17:24, 25, 28 NIV).

The universe is a remarkable evidence of an infinite Creator. Its very existence points to the reality of a powerful God. The Psalmist understood this truth when he wrote, **"The heavens declare the glory of God; the skies proclaim the work of his hands. Day after day they pour forth speech; night after night they display knowledge" (Psalm 19:1, 2 NIV).**

II. COMPELLING TELEOLOGICAL EVIDENCE

The wonder and the beauty of our universe are amazing sights to observe. In every realm we observe compelling evidence of design, purpose, beauty, complexity, and order. This amazing evidence convinced Albert Einstein to make the eloquent remark, **"I cannot believe that God plays dice with the cosmos."**[34] Astrophysicists declare that our planet is incredibly unique in its position, function and existence. It is the right distance from the sun for human life to exist. If it were any closer it would be too hot, if further away it would be too cold. As philosopher J. P. Moreland suggests, **"In the formation of the universe, the balance of matter to antimatter had to be accurate to one part in ten billion for the universe to even arise. Had it been larger or** 19 greater by one part in ten billion, no universe would have arisen."[35]

For many scientists, exposure to the order of the universe, as well as its beauty and complexity, is an occasion of wonder and reverence. Philosopher of science Stanley L. Jaki, referring to the splendor of our universe, observes, "It has supreme coherence from the very small to the very large. It is a consistent unity free of debilitating paradoxes. It is beautifully proportioned into layers or dimensions and yet all of them are in perfect interaction."[36] Even the skeptic David Hume, a renowned critic of the proofs for God's existence, was so impressed by the force of the evidence that he wrote, "A purpose, an intention, or design strikes everywhere the most careless, the most stupid thinker; and no man can be so hardened in absurd systems, as at all times to reject it."[37] One of the greatest minds of science, if not the greatest scientist, Sir Isaac Newton, whose scientific achievements still boggle the modern mind, was a firm believer in the argument from design. The evidence of intricate order and complexity in the universe confirmed his confidence in the existence of an intelligent Designer. He declares, "When I look at the solar system, I see the earth at the right distance from the sun to receive the proper amounts of heat and light. This did not happen by chance."[38]

The evidence from design commonly regarded as the teleological argument is one of the most popular arguments employed by philosophers. The great philosopher Plato observed there are two things that lead people to believe in God: the evidence from the experience of the soul and "from the order of the motion of the stars, and of all things under the dominion of the mind which ordered the universe."[39] Even the great logician Aristotle, who gave us the laws of logic and proposed that philosophy begins with the sense of wonder, was impressed by the wonder of the cosmos. The elegance of this argument is evident in its impact on numerous scientists today. This argument, notes philosopher William Craig, is "the oldest and most popular of all the arguments for the existence of God."[40] Referring to this evidence, the German philosopher Immanuel Kant in his famous work, *Critique of Pure Reason* insists that the argument "always deserves to be mentioned with respect."[41]

The argument from design, in spite of David Hume's earlier critique, has received, as philosopher J. P. Moreland correctly points out, "strong support in recent years from astronomy, physics, and biology."[42] This argument is brilliantly defended by able minds in the rank of Richard Taylor, F. R. Tennant, Richard Swinburne, and A. E. Taylor. Through the centuries great minds like Plato, Aristotle, William Paley, Aquinas, and others have used it.

At the "Christianity Challenges the University: An International Conference of Theists and Atheists," participants trained in natural sciences were asked what particular evidence played an important part in their conversion. Their unanimous response was, "The incredible design or order in the universe was overwhelming evidence for a divine plan and the existence of a Divine Planner."[43] "The principle of teleological purpose," observes Nobel Prize winner Sir Ernst Chain, "stares the biologist in the face wherever he looks."[44] Internationally known Australian cosmologist, Paul Davies, who is the head of theoretical physics at the University of Adelaide, declares, "It is hard to resist the impression that the present structure of the universe, apparently so sensitive to minor alterations in the numbers, has been rather carefully thought out . . . the seemingly miraculous concurrence of these numerical values must remain the most compelling evidence for cosmic design."[45]

Recent scientific observation is providing supporting evidence in the light of what scientists presently call the "anthropic principle" in cosmology. Astrophysicists suggest that life in our universe would not be possible if the early condition of the universe had varied even slightly. The universe appears to be designed for life. In other words, it is "fine-tuned" for our existence. The brilliant scientist Stephen W. Hawking observes, "If the rate of expansion one second after the big bang had been smaller by even one part in a hundred thousand million million, the universe would have re-collapsed before it even reached its present size."[46] Philosopher John Leslie argues that the anthropic principle provides an excellent defense for the design argument. In his work, *The Probability of God,* Hugh Montefiore offers compelling evidence of a designed universe, including the anthropic principle. He claims that chance and natural selection do not offer adequate explanation for the reality of life. God is, notes Montefiore, "by far the most probable explanation."

Consider the following popular analogy provided by New York

University philosopher Richard Taylor.[47] Imagine that you are traveling to Wales by train and as you approach your destination, you observe at the border on a hillside the words "Welcome to Wales" arranged out of white stones. What is the chance of these stones popping out of the earth by themselves, developing a white exterior by chance and then rolling together to spell out the words "Welcome to Wales"? In reality the complexity that we observe in our cosmos is far greater than the simple sign "Welcome to Wales." It is more probable mathematically speaking, for those stones by blind chance to emerge out of the ground, develop a white exterior, roll down and form the words "Welcome to Wales" than for chance evolution to produce the complexity we observe in the universe.

It is eminently more reasonable to believe that our universe is the product of intelligent design than it is to perceive that it is a product of chance. Who in his right mind would think that an explosion in a printing shop could produce the *Oxford Dictionary*? Chance has no real basis for producing anything. The assumption that time plus matter plus chance could produce intelligence is mythological. Things don't just come by chance. The idea of chance is meaningless and has no rational or factual support, hence it is logically fallacious. Chance can never be a causal agent for anything. It is not an entity, nor is it a being, but it is a conceptual ambiguity which has no real existence, therefore it is not capable of producing anything. Even a passionate atheist like Richard Dawkins admits, **"The more statistically improbable a thing is, the less we can believe that it just happened by blind chance.**

Superficially, the obvious alternative to chance is an intelligent Designer."[48] Philosopher Norman Geisler concludes, "There may be some theoretical chance that wind and rain erosion could produce the faces of four presidents on the side of a mountain, but it is still far more reasonable to assume that an intelligent sculptor created Mount Rushmore."[49] Theologian Clark Pinnock affirms, "The adaptive harmony we see in the world is meant to be a signal to us about the existence of a Creator."[50]

Although critics have frequently argued that the teleological argument has been conclusively refuted by Hume and Kant, a careful study of the arguments proves otherwise. Philosophers of the caliber of Thomas Reid, F. R. Tennant, A. E. Taylor, Stewart Hackett, Frederick Copleston, Charles H. Malik, Hugo Meynell, and others have cogently responded to Hume's skepticism. It is worth noting that Hume and Kant were not unbiased minds looking at the facts objectively. Their objections were often based on systems which are generally refuted and rejected by many modern philosophers. As philosopher Charles H. Malik observes, "Hume and Kant did not conclude their scepticism and criticism from their rational investigations"[51] but from philosophical presuppositions which are highly questionable, and which if accepted would undermine their own philosophical conclusions; furthermore, few philosophers share their presuppositions.

It is worth noting that while Hume is often perceived as a skeptic, his comment on the famous *Dialogues* suggests otherwise. In the *Dialogues* Philo is the skeptic, Demea the pantheist, and Cleanthes a theist who argues in favor of the teleological evidence. Hume gives his own verdict on the matter, "I confess that, upon a serious review of the whole, I cannot but think that Philo's principles are more probable than Demea's; but that those of Cleanthes approach still nearer to the truth."[52] The evidence of design in the universe provides adequate grounds for affirming the existence of an intelligent Creator.

After returning from his unforgettable flight around the moon with Apollo 8, astronaut Frank Borman was questioned by a reporter. The reporter pointed out that the Soviet cosmonaut who recently returned from space flight said that he did not see God or angels on his flight. "Did you see God?" questioned the reporter. To this complex question Frank Borman gave a brilliant response, "No, I did not see him either, but I saw his evidence."

David correctly states, "In the beginning you laid the foundations of the earth, and the heavens are the work of your hands" (Psalm 102:25 NIV).

III. CONSCIOUS MORAL EVIDENCE

A compelling evidence that points to the existence of God is our moral experience. Morality is an essential part of our human fabric. At the conclusion of his famous work, *Critique of Practical Reason*, Immanuel Kant proposed a new argument for the existence of God called "the moral argument."[53] Kant declares, "Two things fill the mind with ever new and increasing admiration and awe . . . the starry heavens above me and the moral law within me."[54] Plato long before Kant argued that the concept of goodness makes good sense only in relation to the greater or the ultimate good.[55]

If God exists, it would be natural to expect his created beings to experience moral convictions. No human existence is possible without subscribing to moral values. Every day we observe politicians, doctors, lawyers, psychologists, judges, sociologists, editors, police, and citizens arguing for justice, fairness, equality, tolerance, honesty, responsibility, duty, accountability, civil rights, human rights, women's rights, etc. We believe it is right to treat all people with equal right. We condemn racism, rape, violence, child abuse, war, corruption, murder, treason, betrayal, abortion, and other behavior as evil and wrong. The reality of our moral commitment and conscience is unavoidable: we live in a moral universe.

Every individual appeals to a moral law by which he/she makes moral judgements. Our moral standards provide a basis for our thinking and behavior. But what about the relativist who insists there are no absolutes and argues everything is relative? Those who reject absolute moral law and advocate relativism engage in promoting a belief which is logically self-contradictory, subjective, and arbitrary. The rejection of absolutes in an important sense is the death of morals, where the individual becomes morally paralyzed and unable to make a distinction between good and evil, right and wrong. The suggestion that there are no absolutes is in fact an absolute position. It is self-contradictory for someone to say, "I am absolutely sure that there are no absolutes!" It does not remove absolutes but seductively substitutes itself as the guiding principle. Like the statements: There are no rules; Trust no authority; Everything is relative; All beliefs are false, each affirmation becomes an absolute in itself, which is what the person wishes to deny. Hence it is not only self-refuting but arbitrary and meaningless. This type of thinking can be seen in the ancient Greek saying, "Every statement is a lie!"

and the Zen Buddhist aphorism, "All statements are absurd!" To reject moral absolutes is in essence to affirm that there are no real differences between Mother Teresa and Hitler.

Relativism may appear impressive on the surface, but it is philosophically false. It is logically contradictory, morally inadequate, and existentially unlivable.[56] Consider the true story of a philosophy student who wrote an ethics paper arguing that there are no absolutes and everything is relative. Judged by the research, documentation, and scholarship, the paper deserved an "A". The professor, however, gave it an "F" with a note explaining, "I do not like blue covers!" When the student received his paper, he was so upset that he stormed into the professor's office protesting, "This is not fair! This is not just! I shouldn't be graded on the color of the cover but on the content of my paper."

The professor looked the student in the eye and asked, "Was this the paper which argued that there are no objective moral principles such as fairness and justice and everything is relative to one's taste?"

"Yes! Yes! That's the one," replied the student.

"Well then," said the professor. "I do not like blue covers. The grade will remain an 'F'!" Suddenly the young man understood that moral absolutes are unavoidable, that in fact he believed in moral principles such as fairness and justice, and that furthermore he was expecting them to be applied in his case.

The Cambridge scholar C. S. Lewis writes, "If no set of moral ideas were truer or better than any other, there would be no sense in preferring civilised morality to savage morality, or Christian morality to Nazi morality." Thus he says:

■ **The moment you say that one set of moral ideas can be better than another, you are, in fact, measuring them both by a standard, saying that one of them conforms to that standard more nearly than the other.**[57]

The reality of this universal law is very much part of our human fabric. We are not merely mechanical beings. Our moral convictions are essential to our existence; without them we would hardly qualify to be human, as Henry M. Morris plainly explains:

■ **Each individual, however benighted, recognises something in him that tells him that he ought to do the thing that is right morally and ought to shun the wrong – even though individual standards as to what constitutes right and wrong seem to vary somewhat with time and place.**[58]

An interesting episode at an eastern United States university illustrates this truth remarkably. A professor informed his students, before their exam, to sit one seat apart so that they may avoid all appearance of evil "as the Good Book says."

"What if we don't believe in the Good Book?" asked a skeptical student.

"Then you put two seats between you," replied the professor. Point well made. Without morals life is unlivable.

Are our moral values merely sociological conventions similar to driving on the left versus right side of the road or like subjective utterances that we produce when we order our meals in a restaurant? If morality is merely social conventions, then it is not objective or absolute. In this case the logical question would be, why follow the subjective opinions of society? Why should anyone sacrifice for another's well being? What if society approves cannibalism, ritual human sacrifice, or racism? Morals cannot be the basis of instinct, for there is a law within us that judges between our instincts and what we decide that we should obey. Philosopher C. Stephen Evans notes, **"Morality is not simply a law of nature like the law of gravity. It doesn't describe how things in nature go on, but how human behavior ought to go on."**[59] The moral law is not descriptive "is" (state of being) but prescriptive "ought" (something we ought to do). It is not something physical but metaphysical. Moral philosophers have correctly argued that the prescriptive "ought" can never be derived from a descriptive "is." The brilliant philosopher Ludwig Wittgenstein pointed out that the basis of morality and ethics comes from outside the human situation. **"Ethics, if it is anything,"** he wrote, **"is supernatural."**[60] In essence morality is transcendental. If our universe affirms the reality of a moral law and we are creatures with moral capacities, then it is logical to assume that God must exist as a moral Being capable of ensuring justice. The English idealist philosopher Hasting Rashdall's insight on the problem is remarkable. He logically concludes:

■ **A moral ideal can exist nowhere and nohow but in a Mind; an absolute moral ideal can exist only in a Mind from which all Reality is derived. Our moral ideal can only claim objective validity in so far as it can rationally be regarded as the revelation of a moral ideal eternally existing in the mind of God.**[61]

If the moral law is not from God, then one must conclude that it evolved from non-moral matter. But the concept of an evolving morality is just a tautology. Morality cannot simply evolve or change. People's idea of morality may change, but morality itself is unchangeable; like the laws of logic and mathematics, it is the law of reality. Something is either right or wrong, good or evil. It is never right to kill an innocent person. It is always wrong to abuse a child whether today or twenty years from now.

It would be unreasonable to argue, as did the lady from London that C. S. Lewis once wrote about, "I don't worry if there is a shortage of bread in our town, because in our home we only eat toast." It is equally irrational to think that we could have objective moral law without an objective moral law giver. If there is no God, there is no logical ground for our morality. The

"When we try to think about this infinitely fascinating universe in which we live we find that we are faced in the end with the mystery of existence, of why there is a universe at all."
John Hick, philosopher

humanist philosopher Paul Kurtz argues cogently when he states, "The central question about moral and ethical principles concerns this ontological foundation. If they are neither derived from God nor anchored in some transcendent ground, are they purely ephemeral?"[62] Kurtz concedes that if ethics are not theistic they are transient, ephemeral, and temporal. The rejection of God logically implies the elimination of absolute morality. Richard Taylor, an eminent ethicist from New York, observes, "The modern age, more or less repudiating the idea of a divine lawgiver, has nevertheless tried to retain the ideas of moral right and wrong, not noticing that, in casting God aside, they have also abolished the conditions of meaningfulness for moral right and wrong as well."[63]

The point of the argument is that our moral experience points to a transcendent God who is the source and ground of our morality. If this is not the case, then the alternative is devastating, as the British theologian D. M. Baillie rightly suggests, "Either our moral values tell us something about the nature and purpose of reality . . . or they are subjective and therefore meaningless."[64] This conclusion is logically sound. If our morality is not grounded in God, then it is hopelessly subjective. But to reject moral values as meaningless is logically impossible and existentially inadequate. Those who argue that morality is simply descriptive rather than prescriptive miss the point. If morality is nothing more than what humans have invented, then our moral behavior is simply arbitrary and has no ultimate meaning, significance, or value. Very few can meaningfully and consistently live on this assumption.

An excellent case in point is the French atheistic existentialist Jean-Paul Sartre, who rejected morality as meaningless but could not live on the basis of that rejection. He said, "If God does not exist, we find no values or commands to turn to which legitimize our conduct. So, in the bright realm of values, we have no excuse behind us, nor justification before us. We are alone, with no excuses."[65] After denying the objectivity of morality, Sartre went against his view by signing the Algerian Manifesto (1960) which declared that the Algerian war was wrong. In other words, Sartre could not live with his atheistic existentialism. If there is an objective moral law then there must be a moral law-giver. David Elton Trueblood puts it, "The recognition of an objective moral law drives us to the belief in God."[66]

Our moral reality provides a crucial clue to the meaning of the universe. In the words of the famous New York scholar Peter Berger, our moral factors are *"signals of transcendence within the . . . human condition."*[67] The apostle Paul, writing to the Christians in Rome, confirms the reality of the moral evidence, "Since they show that the requirements of the law are written on their hearts, their consciences also bearing witness, and their thoughts now accusing, now even defending them" (Romans 2:15 NIV).

IV. CONCRETE CHRISTOLOGICAL EVIDENCE

A number of contemporary scholars insist that one of the greatest evidences for the existence of God is the reality of Jesus Christ. There is something incredibly remarkable that we discover in the life and actions of Jesus. The noted theoretical physicist Dr. John Polkinghorne, a former colleague of Stephen Hawking and a scholar known for his brilliance in his field, after looking at the evidence for Christ, observes, "The reason why I take my stand within the Christian community lies in certain events which took place in Palestine nearly two thousand years ago."[68] The Christological evidence cannot be simply dismissed as a religious fabrication. To do so is to pre-judge the case. A sensible approach would be to examine the facts, weigh the evidence, ask some tough questions, then reach a reasonable conclusion in the light of existing evidence. A number of skeptics including Frank Morison, C. S. Lewis, John Warwick Montgomery, Josh McDowell, and Simon Greenleaf have taken this approach and been overwhelmed by the evidence.[69]

Rousseau, the French philosopher, writes, "Yes, if the life and death of Socrates are those of a philosopher, the life and death of Jesus Christ are those of a God."[70] As we approach this evidence it is worth noting that we are moving from the ideal to the real, from the abstract to the concrete, from the invisible to the visible. It is absolutely impossible to explain Jesus apart from the fact that he was from God. The American theologian Loraine Boettner puts it well:

■ **Nothing is more clear than that Christ cannot be explained by any humanistic system. He does not fit into any theory of natural evolution, for in that case the perfect flower of** humanity should have appeared at the end of human history and not in the middle of it.[71]

According to Arnold Toynbee, the famous English historian, "Jesus Christ will still be important for mankind two or three thousand years hence."[72] Jesus Christ is a fact of history. To ignore him is to ignore history. H. G. Wells, the Oxford historian, in his popular book, *The Outline of History*, makes this remark, "Here was a man. This part of the tale could not have been invented."[73] And we cannot escape the logic of St. Anselm, "Jesus is either God or he is not good." C. S. Lewis argues along the same line:

■ **The discrepancy between the depth and sanity . . . of His moral teaching and the rampant megalomania which must lie behind His theological teaching unless He is indeed God, has never been satisfactorily explained. Hence the non-Christian hypotheses succeed one another with the restless fertility of bewilderment.[74]**

The biblical evidence indicates that Christ claims to be the Son of God, God in human form, equal to God, sinless as God, with authority to forgive sin, to grant eternal life, to be worthy of worship and to be the truth. John Warwick Montgomery declares, "We may not like the Jesus of the historical documents; but like him or not, we meet him there as a divine being on whom our personal destiny depends."[75] The claims of Christ are unique compared to the claims of all the religious founders of the world. Mohammed never claimed to be God; Buddha remained silent on the question of God; Confucius refused to discuss the idea of God; Moses merely claimed to be a prophet of God. Only Jesus claimed to be God incarnate.

When one considers the claims of Christ, there are several points worth reflecting upon:

- First, his claims are consistent with his life.
- Second, his claims are consistent with the entire revelation of God – general and special (written).
- Third, his claims are consistent with the reality in which man lives.
- Fourth, his claims are consistent with our religious experience.
- Fifth, his claims are consistent with his resurrection.

If we reject the claims of Christ, how do we account for his resurrection? One of Christ's biographers writes, "After his suffering, he showed himself to these men and gave many convincing proofs that he was alive. He appeared to them over a period of forty days and spoke about the kingdom of God" (Acts 1:3 NIV). The apostle Paul writing to the Romans reveals a significant truth about Christ. He states Christ "was declared with power to be the Son of God by his resurrection from the dead: Jesus Christ our Lord" (Romans 1:4 NIV).

The resurrection of Christ in a remarkable way demonstrates the deity of Christ. In essence the resurrection is the foundation of Christianity. Without it Christianity has no ground for belief. The significant question is, "Did the resurrection really happen?" It is reasonable to conclude that if the resurrection took place, Jesus Christ is by far the most important person in history. There are three major evidences that support the historicity of the resurrection.

I. THE EMPTY TOMB

One significant evidence for the resurrection is the empty tomb. The disciples of Jesus observed that the tomb was empty after the resurrection. The Gospels affirm that at least six of Christ's followers saw the empty tomb:

Mary Magdalene (Matthew 28:1–10); Mary (the mother of James) and Salome (Mark 16:1–8); Joanna (Luke 24:10); Peter and John (John 20:2–8). The Roman guards also saw the empty tomb (Matthew 28:2,11–15). The Jews never denied it and Peter proclaimed the resurrection to 3,000 people who could have refuted it. It is difficult to dismiss the evidence for the empty tomb.

According to D. H. Van Daalen, "It is extremely difficult to object to the empty tomb on historical grounds; those who deny it do so on the basis of theological or philosophical assumptions."[76] There are more than fifty reputable scholars who accept the evidence for the empty tomb.[77] J. A. T. Robinson states, "The recent mythological view fails to do justice to the scriptural evidence. Many in fact will continue to find it easier to believe that the empty tomb produced the disciples' faith than that the disciples' faith produced the empty tomb."[78]

2. THE APPEARANCES OF CHRIST

Luke writes, "He showed himself to these men and gave many convincing proofs that he was alive. He appeared to them over a period of forty days and spoke about the kingdom of God" (Acts 1:3 NIV). The belief in the resurrection is based not simply on an empty tomb but rather on a living encounter with a risen Lord. The disciples of Christ persisted in their remarkable claim that they saw the living Christ, even under persecution, torture, and death. We cannot dismiss the resurrection experience on the basis of vision or hallucination, for they are insufficient to explain the disciples' revolutionary transformation. This significant fact is vital to the case for the resurrection. Their unique testimony is powerful evidence that their message is trustworthy.

The facts demonstrate that on several occasions different individuals and groups saw Jesus alive after his death. He was seen not only by believers but also by skeptics, unbelievers, and even enemies. The New Testament records twelve separate post-resurrection appearances of Christ. He appeared to: Mary Magdalene (John 20:11); Mary Magdalene and the other Mary (Matthew 28:1); Peter (Luke 24:34); the two disciples (Luke 24:13–32); the eleven apostles (Luke 24:33); Thomas and the other apostles (John 20:26–29); the seven apostles (John 21); all the apostles (Matthew 28:16–20; Acts 1:4–9); the 500 brethren (1 Corinthians 15:6); James (1 Corinthians 15:7); and Paul (1 Corinthians 15:8). Dr. Yandall Woodfin offers an insightful note:

■ **If the early followers had made up the stories, they had little to gain but outward persecution and a lifelong battle with guilt. It seems more reasonable to believe, rather, that**

hypocrites do not become good martyrs and that the resurrection happened.[79]

The questions which we must face if we reject their testimony are, why would the disciples lie and what would they gain by lying about the event? This would be a greater miracle indeed.

3. THE ORIGIN OF THE CHRISTIAN FAITH

The origin of the church proves the resurrection. What gave birth to the church? Why and how did the church come into being? What persuaded the early Jewish believers to put their faith in Jesus Christ? Scholars agree that Christianity came into being because the disciples believed that God had raised Jesus from the dead. Something dramatic took place in Jerusalem which has altered human history. What caused the disciples to believe and preach the resurrection? It was the fact of the resurrection. (Acts 2:32, 36; 13:26–39; 17:22–34; Romans 1:4; 14:9; 1 Thessalonians 4:14). The apostle Paul clearly states, "And if Christ has not been raised, our preaching is useless and so is your faith" (1 Corinthians 15:14). If the resurrection is not true, there is no eternal life, and all who trust in Christ are in fact lost. To deny the evidence of the resurrection would require far greater faith than to believe it. Outside of the resurrection there is no logical explanation for the origin of the Christian church. The objections against the resurrection have been adequately answered by a number of scholars including Charles Anderson, Raymond Brown, William Lane Craig, James D. G. Dunn, F. X. Durrwell, M. Green, Gary Habermas, Murray Harris, G. E. Ladd, F. Morison, James Orr, Grant Osborne, Wolfhart Pannenberg, W. J. Sparrow-Simpson, John W. Wenham, and others.

Professor C. F. D. Moule of Cambridge University insists that the origin

of Christianity must "remain an unsolved enigma for any historian who refuses to take seriously the only explanation offered by the Church itself."[80] According to Professor Moule, nothing can adequately explain the origin of Christianity outside the resurrection event. If the resurrection is true, then we don't have to speculate on the meaning of life. We have something concrete on which to base our trust and hope. In the resurrection of Christ, God has demonstrated to the world that there is a purpose to life and ultimate hope for our existence beyond the grave. The resurrection reveals that God is not a cosmic executive gone away on a long distance trip, but a gracious loving Father compassionately seeking for his lost people.

Thomas Arnold, who held the chair of Modern History at Oxford University and was noted for his famous three-volume *History of Rome*, declares:

> ■ **I know of no one fact in the history of mankind which is proved by better and fuller evidence of every sort, to the understanding of a fair inquirer, than the great sign which God has given us that Christ died and rose again from the dead.[81]**

No theory has ever been formed which could logically refute the reality of the resurrection while carefully observing all the evidence.

All the above evidences confirm that God really exists and that there is enough evidence for a man who wants to believe, but there is no evidence for a man who refuses to believe. The conclusion of Pascal is most appropriate, "The evidence of God's existence and His gift is more than compelling, but those who insist that they have no need of Him or it will always find ways to discount the offer."[82]

A teacher once told her students to produce a painting. Nearly all the pic-

tures were vaguely human except the one produced by a boy named Tommy. "What's that?" inquired the teacher, observing a peculiar mass of color.

"It's God!" replied the youngster.

"But no one knows what God is like," said the teacher.

The boy looked up with an air of confidence and a sense of triumph, "Now they do!" This is precisely what the disciples said about Jesus Christ. "No one has ever seen God, but God the One and Only, who is at the Father's side, has made him known" (John 1:18 NIV). By the light of the sun we see the world, but by the brilliance of Christ we see God. In the ocean of darkness, Christ shines as a beacon of light. The apostle Paul understood this truth when he wrote, "For God, who said, 'Let light shine out of darkness,' made his light shine in our hearts to give us the light of the knowledge of the glory of God in the face of Christ" (2 Corinthians 4:6 NIV).

If there is no God
it would be necessary to invent him.

VOLTAIRE

God whispers to us
in our pleasures, speaks in
our conscience, but shouts in
our pains: it is His megaphone
to rouse a deaf world.

C. S. LEWIS

The world is all the richer
for having a Devil in it, so long as
we keep our foot upon his neck.

WILLIAM JAMES

IF THERE IS A GOD, WHY IS THERE EVIL?

2

NOTHING disturbs our existence more than the tragic reality of evil. Indeed, the trouble that troubles humanity is trouble. No one escapes it or can ignore it. The reality of evil touches every level of our lives. Its existence staggers our minds and moves our hearts. Pain, cruelty, calamities, injustices, and death disturb us and leave us helpless. How frequently one hears statements like, "I believed in God until my child was killed in an accident." "Why do the innocent suffer?" "Why are babies born blind and many maimed for life?"

If there is a God, why did he allow Hitler, Stalin, Idi Amin, and Pol Pot to murder the innocent? If God exists, how could he allow these tragic wars? These are pressing questions which every reflective and sensitive mind frequently ponders – questions which we must face both intellectually and existentially.

Various philosophers have debated over the question of evil; theologians have proposed a variety of solutions, and skeptics frequently rely on it to advance their unbelief. Disturbed by its reality, Stendhal declares, "God's only excuse is that he does not exist."[1] Thomas Huxley was even more adamant, "If our hearing were sufficiently acute to catch every note of pain, we would be deafened by one continuous scream."[2] Particularly striking are the remarks of the British philosopher Bertrand Russell:

> ■ **I would invite any Christian to accompany me to the children's ward of a hospital, to watch the suffering that is there being endured, and then to persist in the assertion that those children are so morally abandoned as to deserve what they are suffering.[3]**

According to Russell, no one could sit beside a dying child and still believe in the existence of God. After wrestling with the reality of evil, Nobel prize winner Albert Camus concluded, "The final philosophical question is the question of suicide."[4]

In his famous novel, *The Plague*, Camus has a striking scene where a priest, an unbeliever, and a doctor surround the bed of a little boy dying of bubonic plague. As the boy suffers in pain, the priest asks God for help, "God, spare the child." But tragically the boy dies. Later, in the hospital garden, the priest declares, "That sort of thing is revolting because it passes human understanding, but perhaps we should try to love what we cannot understand." The doctor, hearing this, shouts, "No, Father! I have a very different idea of love and until my dying day I refuse to believe in a God who lets a child die like that."[5]

In an important public debate several years ago, the atheist Charles Smith passionately illustrated the problem for those who believe in the existence of a good God:

> ■ **A few years ago in Arizona a mother and child were left alone on a ranch. The father had gone away. A rattlesnake**

bit the mother. She tried to get help, but was far distant from the nearest human being. What could she do? She saw she was going to die and that the children would starve, as the father would not return for a week. She killed her baby and herself. How can you explain such an event if God exists?[6]

The existence of evil is indeed one of the greatest obstacles to belief in God. It is without a doubt the most intellectually challenging of all objections. Evangelical philosopher Elton Trueblood notes, "It is a problem which no theist can avoid and no honest thinker will try to avoid."[7] James Orr insists, "The problem of evil is one of the most crucial protests raised by unbelievers against the fact of God."[8] The process philosopher Alfred North Whitehead writes, "All simplifications of religious dogma are shipwrecked upon the rock of the problem of evil."[9] The British writer John W. Wenham was not exaggerating when he said, "Evil constitutes the biggest single argument against the existence of an almighty, loving God."[10] Hugh Silvester looks at the problem from another angle, "If God knew that certain of His creatures were destined to an eternal sentence in hell, we may ask why He created them at all."[11] In the light of this problem, the modern poet Robert Hale concludes, "If you give me a choice between voting for 'God is dead' or 'Everything (including evil) is God's will,' I would have to abstain."[12]

The reality of evil confronts every philosophy of life, and the burden of explaining its origin and existence lies equally upon all. It is not a problem unique to the Christian faith, as R. C. Sproul has so aptly observed, "Indeed, every philosophical theory has to deal with it in some way."[13] However, in theological circles the problem is treated very poorly, as the American philosopher Brand Blanshard states in his extremely significant volume, *Reason and Belief*, "The treatment of evil by theology seems to me an intellectual disgrace."[14] Ed. L. Miller insists, "The theologian's inability to supply the skeptic with a straightforward and satisfying answer to this challenge has made evil, no doubt, the biggest single stumbling block to belief in a God of love."[15] Although this may be an overstatement, there are excellent insights one could gain from the reflections of theologians.

What are we to make of evil? How shall we respond to this pressing problem? Does the existence of pain and suffering deny the existence of God? Does he care for the suffering of mankind? Is he interested in our pain and grief? In what sense is the existence of evil incompatible with the existence of God? If there is a God, why is there evil? These are important questions and they deserve our deepest reflection. If we avoid these questions, then we have nothing to say to a troubled world!

There are a number of approaches to the problem, but space will not allow us to treat all the attempted solutions. We will limit our discussion to a number of fundamental factors. From a contemporary point of view there are generally three main responses to this problem: atheism, eastern religion, and Christianity.

I. ATHEISTIC CONFUSION

Atheists frequently argue that the presence of evil in the world is incompatible with the nature of God's existence. Atheists, such as Antony Flew, George H. Smith, Woolsey Teller, Kai Nielson, Michael Martin, Richard R. LaCroix, and others, offer several arguments from the problem of evil against the existence of God.

The most famous version of the argument comes from the Greek philosopher Epicurus, who sums up the indictment as, **"Either He is not good, or else He is not almighty."** David Hume, the skeptical philosopher, states the same argument with much clarity:

■ **Is he (God) willing to prevent evil, but not able? Then he is impotent. Is he able, but not willing? Then he is malevolent. Is he both able and willing? Whence then is evil?**[16]

Epicurus (341–270 B.C.) first stated this problem and later was quoted by Lactanitus (A.D. 260–340). The problem could be expressed in the following logical diagram:

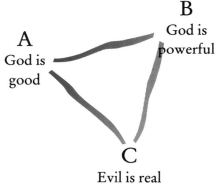

B
God is
powerful

A
God is
good

C
Evil is real

Theists believe (A) God is good and (B) God is powerful, but the problem is, how do we explain (C) in the light of A and B? There are a number of possible explanations as to why evil exists.[17] Christian thinkers provide the following reasons:

1. The existence of Satan who is often responsible for evil actions.
2. The eschatological explanation that God's final defeat of evil will demonstrate God's omnipotence.

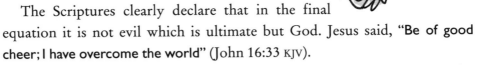

3. The concepts of punishment and retribution, which are further reasons for the existence of evil.
4. The idea of discipline for wrongdoing, which provides insight into the meaning of evil.
5. The concept of probation, which also makes some sense in the light of evil.
6. The idea that suffering can be a means of revelation to understand God.
7. The concept of redemption, which makes sense in the light of evil.

The Scriptures clearly declare that in the final equation it is not evil which is ultimate but God. Jesus said, "Be of good cheer; I have overcome the world" (John 16:33 KJV).

Thomas Aquinas, the brilliant medieval philosopher, recognized the problem of evil and offered the following response:

■ **For because we have proven that every agent acts insofar as it acts through God's power, with God being thus the cause of all effects and acts, and since we proved that evil and defects in beings directed by divine providence come from the condition of the secondary causes, which themselves may be defective, it is obvious that evil actions, understood as defective, do not originate from God but from their defective proximate causes.[18]**

Several Christian philosophers have adequately responded to this dilemma. The works of C. S. Lewis, Alvin C. Plantinga, John Hick, M. B. Ahern, Norman L. Geisler, Austin Farrer, Nelson Pike, Michael L. Peterson, and others, offer excellent replies to the charges of atheists.

The popular argument of the atheist carries little weight and is self-refuting. The argument could be stated as follows:

1. There is evil in the world,
2. evil is incompatible with God,
3. therefore God does not exist.

C. S. Lewis, a former atheist who rejected the existence of God on the basis of the existence of evil, asserts, "My argument against

God was that the universe seemed so cruel and unjust."[19] The objection is logically fallacious. It misses the truth at several points. Firstly, the skeptics presuppose subjectively without a proof that evil is incompatible with the existence of God. This premise is presumed, not proven. The skeptic must prove his assumption in order to validate his argument. Secondly, it is still logically possible that God in his wisdom may allow evil for a very good purpose, and for some wise reason he has not disclosed that truth. Unless the skeptic has all the reason on the matter and is able to offer good reason that it is the case, the skeptic is indeed rather premature to conclude that the existence of evil is incompatible with God. A logical response to the atheistic argument is:

1. God is omnipotent;
2. God is benevolent;
3. since God is not yet finished with the world,
4. evil will remain until God eliminates it.

William Dyrness is right, "Many people who do not believe in God seem to bear a great resentment against Christians and against God for a problem which on their own assumptions does not exist at all."[20] The

fact of evil in no way eliminates the reality of God. Thus, as Arlie J. Hoover rightly points out, "If we don't know his reason for evil this is very interesting philosophically and psychologically, but hardly a contradiction."[21] To charge this as a contradiction, Hoover says,

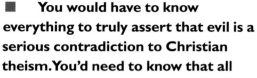

■ **You would have to know everything to truly assert that evil is a serious contradiction to Christian theism. You'd need to know that all proposed harmonies are false. You'd have to establish propositions like, "God would *never* allow suffering," or "God would have created *only* blessed men." Can any man really prove such propositions as these? How? How would one know so much about what God could or would do?**[22]

The obvious fallacy in the argument from evil is that of "begging the question." In "begging the question" the person does not prove his point but merely moves in a circle and states the same point twice. This fallacy fails to support the very question at issue. For example, a circular definition would be, "A morally good man is one who acts virtuously." Another common one is, "It is better to be idle than to do nothing." Atheists argue from a premise which their philosophy denies. Jean-Paul Sartre poignantly suggests the atheistic position, "The existentialist (atheist) finds it extremely embarrassing that God does not exist, for there disappears with Him all possibility of finding value in an intelligible heaven."[23]

In his work, *Existentialism and Humanism*, Sartre agrees with Dostoyevsky, "If God did not exist, everything would be permitted."[24] Strictly from an atheistic context there are no absolutes, everything is relative; there is no ultimate law of morals, everything is subjective. If there is no God, there is no absolute moral standard by which to determine what is good or evil. C. S. Lewis effectively points out the difficulty of maintaining absolute standards and principles in a human society:

■ **Unless we take our own standard of goodness to be valid in principle (however fallible our particular applications of it) we cannot mean anything by calling waste and cruelty evils. And unless we take our own standard to be something more than ours, to be in fact an objective principle to which we are responding, we cannot regard that standard as valid. In a word, unless we all consider ultimate reality to be moral, we cannot morally condemn it.[25]**

Philosopher David Freeman argues rightly, "The point is that unless moral standards have the approval and sanction of God, unless God is the moral lawgiver, there are no unchanging moral standards."[26] In the same vein, British neo-Thomastic philosopher Eric Mascall observes:

■ **If there is no God, then there is no problem of reconciling the existence of pain and sin with his love and power; and, while the atheist may with reason urge against theism that it has set itself a problem which it cannot solve, he has no business to feel evil as constituting a problem for him, except in the purely intellectual sense of causing him to wonder where it came from.[27]**

C. S. Lewis argues with irrefutable logic in his popular volume, *Mere Christianity*, the fallacy of arguing against God on the basis of evil. He writes:

■ **Thus in the very act of trying to prove that God did not exist – in other words, that the whole of reality was senseless – I found I was forced to assume that one part of reality – namely my idea of justice – was full of sense. Consequently atheism turns out to be too simple.[28]**

Atheists stand on a moral principle and charge God for breaking this principle. The point is, where did this principle come from? Not from society, for what is a society but a group of individuals, and we don't get principles and values just by approaching them. We don't determine truth by counting noses. If society can produce absolute moral standards, then who could argue against Hitler's society for killing the Jews? Philosopher Richard Purtill correctly observes:

■ **If our rationality and morality do not come from God they come from chance permutations of some basic stuff or from the working of mindless forces. In either case, they have no validity.[29]**

The atheistic view of evil is totally inadequate in the light of reality. It is subjective, arbitrary and meaningless. For this important reason the former atheist C. E. M. Joad abandoned his faith in atheism and became a Christian. Professor Joad writes:

■ **To me, at any rate, the view of evil implied by Marxism, expressed by Shaw and maintained by modern psychotherapy, a view which regards evil as the by-product of circumstances which circumstances can, therefore, alter and even eliminate, has come to seem intolerably shallow.[30]**

What is most interesting is that atheists appear to be very resentful toward the reality of evil even though, according to their world-view, there is no one to be resentful against. Mascall points out, "This is very mysterious, and almost leads one to suspect that the atheists have been indulging in a little surreptitious theism on the quiet."[31] Thus, the fact of human moral experience points to the reality of God – not to its negation. F. J. Sheed says:

■ **Suffering would be altogether intolerable if there were no God....Atheism answers that the fact of suffering proves that there is no God. But this does not reduce the world's sufferings by one hair-breadth, it only takes away hope.**[32]

The famous English apologist John Henry Newman was speaking on this point when he wrote, "I think if this life is the end, and there is no God to wipe away all tears from all eyes, why, I could go mad."[33] Our discussion should not escape the splendid insight of philosopher Ed. L. Miller:

■ **Why is it any easier to account for goodness without God than it is to account for evil with him? That the problem of evil generates more fury than the problem of goodness may be more a matter of psychology than philosophy.**[34]

The most serious fallacy in the atheistic argument is what logicians call "the diversion." The fallacy here is to move away from the central issue to a secondary issue. The point of the matter is that evil has nothing to do with the existence of God. In reality, the problem of evil questions God's character but not his existence. Agreeing to this notion, the British scientist A. E. Wilder-Smith observes with splendid insight:

■ **For the atheist maintains that he sees nothing but contradictions in nature. He, therefore, rejects from his world of ideas any thought of a creator behind nature. However, we dare not forget that even the tiniest island of order in the largest sea of chaos demands a creator of that small remaining order.**[35]

There is no logical necessity to conclude that God does not exist simply on the ground that evil exists. In his brilliant work, *God, Freedom and Evil,* philosopher Alvin Plantinga provides an excellent response to the atheistic confusion:

■ **Why suppose that if God *does* have a good reason for permitting evil, the theist would be the first to know? Perhaps God has a good reason, but that reason is too complicated for us to understand.[36]**

II. PANTHEISTIC ILLUSION

Eastern religions such as Hinduism and Buddhism respond to the problem of evil by denying its actual existence. With its concept of monism, that all diversity is mere illusion and that ultimate reality is both One and Good, eastern religion denies the reality of evil. Following the East, Christian Science likewise rejects the existence of evil as illusory. Its founder Mary Baker Eddy in *Science and Health* states, "Evil is but an illusion, and it has no real basis. Evil is a false belief."[37]

This mode of thinking is transparent in the works of Shakespeare, who wrote, "There is nothing either good or bad, but thinking makes it so."[38] To say there is no evil – only how you feel about it matters – is unrealistic in a world of real pain. At a university meeting some years ago, a pantheistic student challenged me about my views on evil. He objected very strongly to my presentation that evil is real. I gently asked him if it was wrong for me to teach that evil was real. He responded, "Yes!" I then asked, "Is it evil to teach that evil is real?" He had no answer, he was in a dilemma. If he accepted my statement he would have to agree to the reality of evil. If he rejected my statement then he would have to deny his basic premise. His only solution was to reject me as an illusion!

The eastern approach to evil does not solve the problem of evil but rather creates a new one. It is not an answer but an escape from reason. If evil, which is so obvious and evident to our minds, is an illusion, what are we to think of the arguments for the illusion of evil? Should we not also consider them as illusions? If we grant the premise that evil is an illusion, what are we to think of the fact that people consider evil to be real? What about the illusion itself, is that not a genuine evil? Since people are deceived into thinking that evil is real, should not this constitute a serious problem, in which case, a real evil?

This view does not explain the origin of the illusion. It offers no explanation for the apparent reality of evil. Its denial does not remove the presence of evil in the world. To accept this theory is to reject the fact of experience. As Christian apologist Norman L. Geisler logically affirms, "Accepting the illusionist's position demands that one admit that all of life as he experiences it is deceiving him."[39] The eastern poet effectively illustrates the dilemma, "Though evil is an illusion, yet when I sit on a pin and it punctures my skin, I dislike what I fancy I feel." It is one thing to believe that evil is an illusion but quite a different matter to live consistently on this premise. As Dr. Geisler correctly points out:

> ■ Those who believe that evil and the world are illusions do not actually function as if this were so. They may maintain that all is an illusion, but if one were to push them in front of an oncoming bus, they would quickly "warm up" to the reality idea![40]

Sigmund Freud is right, "It would be nice if it were true that no evil existed, but the very fact that men wish it to be so makes this belief highly suspect."[41] Along the same line, Elton Trueblood argues, "If all evil, whether moral, natural or intellectual, is truly illusory, we are foolish

"I think if this life is the end, and there is no God to wipe away all tears from all eyes, why, I could go mad."

John Henry Newman

indeed to fight it; it would be far preferable to forget it."[42]

If evil is an illusion, it is pointless to try to improve the conditions of life. Hence the destitute would be left to starve, the sick left to die, there would be no need to have hospitals, schools, and universities. Learning would cease and a new dark age would descend upon the earth. Thus, we reject this view as inhuman, impossible, and irrational. "It is a Christian conviction," writes William Dyrness, "that evil is permitted by a sovereign God in some way that is ultimately compatible with his goodness."[43] But how do we go about justifying the goodness of God in a world of suffering, pain, and evil?

III. THEISTIC SOLUTION

The Christian answer to the problem of evil (theodicy) is the only adequate solution to the reality of evil in the world. The Christian answer differs significantly from all other belief systems. Biblical revelation sheds considerable light on the subject, and the Christian need not sink into the depths of despair and "kiss his brain good-bye" on this issue.

Since the fact of God's existence is overwhelming, it is indeed foolish to deny his existence on the basis of evil. Rejecting God on the basis of evil is like rejecting your parents because they act in a certain way. A scientist does not give up science because he or she encounters a particular puzzle or a difficult problem. The Christian, says David Elton Trueblood,

■ **Has abundant reason to believe in God in the full theistic sense. If, then, he runs into some difficulty, even a difficulty as great as the problem of evil, he does not, for that reason, give up his faith. The reasons for his faith are so great that they can weather a few storms.**[44]

Evil is commonly spoken of in two senses: natural evil and moral evil. J. Edwin Orr's analogy is useful at this point:

■ **A wayfarer takes shelter under a great rock which, loosened by the rain, comes tumbling down, killing him. That is natural evil. A wayfarer takes shelter in a little hut, but a wicked robber stabs him to death. That is moral evil.**[45]

Historically, evil is understood in terms of the Latin word *negatio*. Evil is defined in negative terms, e.g. ungodly, unrighteous, unhappy, etc. To know what is ungodly we have to understand "godly." C. S. Lewis suggests, "Goodness is, so to speak, itself: badness is only spoiled goodness. And there must be something good first before it can be spoiled." Lewis adds, "Evil is a parasite, not an original thing."[46] Evil is meaningful only with the good; it is contingent and dependent, an absence of good; not a positive quality but a negative. Evil is not a being but a parasite of being. Hence, evil is a bad relationship existing between good things. Norman L. Geisler makes an important point:

■ **Darkness is not nothing; it is the absence of light. Likewise, sickness is the absence of health, and death is the absence of life which belongs to a being. All of these are real lacks. Similarly, evil is just as real, although it has no more being of its own than does darkness or sickness.[47]**

God created human beings with the potential and the capacity to choose good or evil. He created the possibility of evil but not its reality. Thus, God is not the author of evil. As E. J. Carnell observes, **"God is the author of the author of sin, but He cannot be the author of sin itself, for sin is the result of a rebellion against God. Can God rebel against Himself?"[48]** In essence, sin is the abuse of free will, the misuse of what is good. As Augustine reminds us:

■ **The will . . . commits sin when it turns away from immutable and common good, toward its private good, either something external to itself or lower than itself. It turns to its own private good when it desires to be its own master.[49]**

The question which comes immediately to our mind when we start to think along this line is, "Why can't God make men who will not do evil?" But here the power of God is called into question. What one fails to understand on this point is that God could do only that which is logically possible and not the logically absurd, such as create square circles or a stick with only one end. This limitation in no way questions God's power. God's power, says C. S. Lewis:

■ **Means power to do all that is intrinsically possible, not to do the intrinsically impossible. You may attribute miracles to Him, but not nonsense. This is no limit to His power. . . . It remains true that all things are possible with God: the intrinsic impossibilities are not things but nonentities.[50]**

Along the same line Ed. L. Miller writes:

■ **Even an omnipotent God cannot do that which is *logically* impossible; he cannot make a rock so big that he cannot lift it, he cannot make four-sided triangles, he cannot make things both to be and not to be at the same time and in the same respect, and he cannot create something that possesses the full power of being that he himself possesses.[51]**

Can God make free, man who is not free? No! Man who is not free, is not man. If man is free then he is free to choose, but choice logically implies the existence of things to choose between. We agree with Cherbonnier, "Only if man can do evil is there any meaning in doing good." William Dyrness remarks rightly:

■ **It is a Christian conviction that evil can be used in a higher purpose, that suffering produces saintliness. If this is true, then it is possible that God's unwillingness to create a world in which evil is impossible reflects neither on his goodness nor on his power, but flows from his eternal and unchanging purposes.**

He further adds, "Perhaps when we view creation in its totality, we will see evil as a necessary element in the meaning of the whole."[52]

To the question, "Why doesn't God stop evil?" we ask, "How much evil do you want God to stop? If God started stopping evil do you think you would survive till midnight?" No one desires God to interfere with his or her actions. How many of us would like a headache each time we think against God? Which robber wants God to prevent him from stealing? The reformed scholar John Gerstner suggests:

■ **While we do not believe that personal freedom is the ultimate explanation of the origin of evil, we do believe that freedom was the means by which sin did come into the world.[53]**

In the same vein John W. Montgomery adds:

■ **To create only those who "must" (in any sense) choose good is to create automata; and to whisk away evil effects as they are produced is to whisk away evil itself, for an act and its consequences are bound together.[54]**

A world where nothing could go wrong would in fact be a world without God. As V. A. Demant put it, "It would be a kind of infallible clockwork – or it

would be a world in which God left no independence of His control at all."[55] It is because of this reality that former atheists, like Lewis, Schelling, Joad, and others have come to believe in the Christian faith.

The presence of evil has some good purposes, as C. S. Lewis points out, "God whispers to us in our pleasures, speaks in our conscience, but shouts in our pains: it is His megaphone to rouse a deaf world."[56] G. K. Chesterton, the brilliant British writer, provides an eloquent description of human existence defaced by sin and suffering. He states:

■ **According to Christianity, in making it (the world), He set
it free. God had written, not so much a poem, but rather a
play; a play he had planned as perfect, but which had
necessarily been left to human actors and stage-managers,
who had since made a great mess of it.**[57]

In the Christian faith we have a God of amazing love who enters fully
into our human anguish and pain; then in the resurrection he gives us a
pledge that he will one day finally overcome evil:

■ **Now the dwelling of God is with men, and he will live with
them. They will be his people, and God himself will be with
them and be their God. He will wipe every tear from their
eyes. There will be no more death or mourning or crying or
pain, for the old order of things has passed away
(Revelation 21:3–4 NIV).**

What is the ultimate answer to the problem of suffering? Christianity says
the answer is the cross! It is the greatest of all answers to the greatest of all
questions. The Christian message affirms that God did not avoid pain and
suffering but endured it. A skeptic once challenged a minister with a pro-
voking question, "Where was your God when my son was dying?" The
minister thoughtfully replied, "Exactly where, when His Son was dying?"

Dorothy L. Sayers' eloquent remarks on the subject are worthy of our reflection:

■ **For whatever reason God chose to make man as he is – limited and suffering and subject to sorrows and death – He had the honesty and the courage to take His own medicine. Whatever game He is playing with His creation, He has kept His own rules and played fair. He can exact nothing from man that He has not exacted from Himself. He has Himself gone through the whole of human experience, from the trivial irritations of family life and the cramping restrictions of hard work and lack of money to the worst horrors of pain and humiliation, defeat, despair, and death. When He was a man, He played the man. He was born in poverty and died in disgrace and thought it well worthwhile.**[58]

"At the heart of the story stands the cross of Christ," writes John W. Wenham, "where evil did its worst and met its match."[59] Along the same line W. H. T. Gairdner writes, "Against the dark background of man's failure and sin, the Cross shows us the measure of God's passion against evil and the measure of God's passion to redeem His sinful children." He eloquently concludes, "Therefore in the Cross holiness and love, wrath and pity, justice and mercy, meet together, and kiss one another."[60]

E. J. Carnell put this delightfully, "The cross of Christ is God's final answer to the problem of evil because the problem of evil is in the cross itself."[61] It is here we see what God has done about evil. He has taken evil at its most brutal and senseless level and transformed it for our eternal redemption. God himself, in the person of Jesus Christ, went through pain, suffering, and death to redeem us from our eternal suffering. Christ not only endured evil but triumphed over it, as Dorothy Sayers so insightfully puts it: "He did not stop the crucifixion; He rose from the dead."[62]

In the light of this reality, life has purpose and meaning; the cosmos is not chaos. There is ultimate significance: God who created the universe is also able to redeem the universe. Job, who suffered greatly but also understood deeply, said, "I know that my Redeemer lives, and that in the end he will stand upon the earth. And after my skin has been destroyed, yet in my flesh I will see God" (Job 19:25–26 NIV).

CHAPTER 3

When a man
ceases to believe
in God he does not
believe in nothing,
he believes almost in
anything.

G. K. CHESTERTON

A little
philosophy leads
to atheism, depth
in philosophy leads
to God.

FRANCIS BACON

Atheism is a disease of the soul
before it is an error of the mind.

PLATO

IS ATHEISM RATIONAL?

3

I**F there is a God,** why are there atheists? Why do people call themselves atheists? What makes atheism so fashionable these days? There was a time when the thought of atheism aroused unspeakable horror, but today one can find atheists in all walks of life. Philosopher Patrick Masterson, in his popular book, *Atheism and Alienation*, asserts:

■ **For today, on an ever increasing scale, people proclaim themselves to be atheists, not so much because of objections to alleged proofs for the existence of God, but rather because they consider that to affirm the existence of God is to set men at odds within themselves and with one another.**[1]

Atheism is an interesting subject for study. Why are the atheists so passionate and obsessed with the non-being of God? Why do many of them devote a lifetime of religious zeal and commitment to the ideals of atheism? Recent studies on atheism provide fascinating insights.[2]

Atheism rests not on a proven belief but rather on the unsupported assumption that there is no God. Boris Pasternak, who wrote the famous novel, *Dr. Zhivago*, once declared, "I am an atheist who has lost his faith."[3] Atheism is a belief based on an idea. It is a particular conceptual approach to life and the universe.[4]

I. THE ASSUMPTIONS OF ATHEISM

Who is an atheist? An atheist is one who rejects any belief in God. The word "atheism" comes from the Greek word *atheos* meaning "without God" (cf.

Ephesians 2:12). According to the atheistic philosopher Paul Edwards, "An 'atheist' is a person who maintains that there is no God, that is, that the sentence 'God exists' expresses a false proposition."[5] Ludwig Feuerbach says, "The personality of God is nothing else than the projected personality of man."[6] The atheistic philosopher Michael Scriven states, "The atheist may believe there is no God because he thinks the concept is essentially self-contradictory, or meaningless, or because he thinks it is wholly superfluous, or because he thinks it is factually false."[7] Elton Trueblood writes, "The honest atheist is simply a person who has looked out upon the world and has come to believe either that there is no adequate evidence that God is or that there is good evidence that God is not."[8] In her book, *What on Earth is an Atheist?*, Madalyn Murray O'Hair states, "I am an atheist and this means at least: I do not believe there is a god, or any gods, personal or in nature, or manifesting himself, herself, or itself in any way."[9] Robert Blatchford, a British atheist, states a position which is quite typical of most atheists:

■ **I claim that the heavenly Father is a myth; that in the face of a knowledge of life and the world, we cannot reasonably believe in Him. There is no heavenly Father watching tenderly over us, His children. He is the baseless shadow of a wistful human dream.**

I do not believe in a God. The belief in a God is still generally accepted. . . . But, in the light of scientific discoveries and demonstrations, such a belief is unfounded and utterly untenable today.[10]

Theologian Alan Richardson affirms, "Atheism in the sense of the denial of God's existence is a modern phenomenon, intelligible only in a theistic context; it made its appearance in a serious sense during the period of the Enlightenment."[11] The American theologian Harold O. J. Brown suggests, "Atheism as we know it in the West is not merely lack of belief in, but rather an attack on God; only where God has been seen as real and personal can much energy be generated in the cause of rebellion against Him."[12]

Another way of putting it is: an atheist is someone who, after studying Philosophy, Theology, History, Religion, Psychology, Biology, Archaeology, Anthropology, Sociology, etc., and searching every space of the universe, thinks he has found conclusive evidence that God does not exist. He

has inspected the heavenly throne and found it to be empty!

There are many forms of atheism in the philosophical jungles of the twentieth century. There is the mythological atheist, dialectical atheist, semantical atheist, and traditional atheist. The most common of these would be the traditional atheist whose views pose a serious challenge to all who believe in God.

The Dogma of Atheism

There is no God.

There is no objective truth.

There is no ground for reason.

There are no absolute morals.

There is no ultimate value.

There is no ultimate meaning.

There is no eternal hope.

II. THE APOSTLES OF ATHEISM

Every religion has its apostles and prophets, and atheism is no exception. Its high priests, preachers, and prophets are all actively preaching the faith of atheism in every country around the world. The evangelists of atheism are constantly seeking for converts to their denomination. Madalyn Murray O'Hair, the high priestess of atheism, crusaded actively on radio and television and in the universities for the cause of atheism. Her zeal for the myth of God is almost unequalled in comparison with those who believe in the reality of God. Her devotion to atheism caused the United States Supreme Court to rule against prayer and Bible reading in public schools. The popularity of atheism today is largely due to the activities of atheistic philosophers, professors, teachers, editors, journalists, etc. Thus we have apostles of atheism in every walk of life.

The most brilliant of all atheists is certainly Friedrich Nietzsche (1844–1900), who took great pains to express that "God is Dead." His works include: *The AntiChrist, Thus Spoke Zarathustra, Beyond Good and Evil, Ecce Homo,* and *The Genealogy of Morals.* In his book, *The Joyful Wisdom,* Nietzsche states:

■ **The most important of more recent events – that "God is dead," that the belief in the Christian God has become unworthy of belief – already begins to cast its first shadows over Europe.... In fact, we philosophers and "free spirits" feel ourselves irradiated as by a new dawn by the report that the "old God is dead"; our hearts overflow with gratitude, astonishment, presentiment and expectation. At last the horizon seems open once more, granting even that it is not bright; our ships can at last put out to sea in face of every danger; every hazard is again permitted to the discerner; the sea, our sea, again lies open before us; perhaps never before did such an "open sea" exist.[13]**

For Nietzsche the "death of God" means the death of all absolutes, values, and morals. He believed that man can create meaning and significance without any reference to a Transcendent Being. Man is sovereign and self-sufficient to produce his own kingdom. In one of his popular works Nietzsche projects himself as the madman; the death of God leads to madness. In his final existential rejection Nietzsche declares, "But we do not at all want to enter the kingdom of heaven: we have become men – so we want the kingdom of earth."[14]

The German philosopher Ludwig Feuerbach (1804–1872) did much to discredit the existence of God through many of his works and especially through his *The Essence of Christianity*, which is still widely read in academic circles. Religious ideas, according to Feuerbach, are merely the projection of human needs and desires. God is simply personified human wishes. He argues:

■ **Man first of all sees his nature as if out of himself, before he finds it in himself. His own nature is in the first instance contemplated by him as that of another being.... Hence the historical progress of religion consists in this: that what by an earlier religion was regarded as objective, is now recognized as subjective; that is, what was formerly contemplated and worshipped as God is now perceived to be something human.[15]**

Two individuals who picked up Feuerbach's atheistic ideas are Sigmund Freud (1856–1939) and Karl Marx. Freud applied Feuerbach's ideas in the field of psychology. His work, *The Future of an Illusion*, affirms that the idea of God is nothing but wish fulfillment, an infantile neurosis for a cosmic comforter. God is an illusory projection of the human mind, removed from truth and reality, hence the enlightened person will abandon the idea of God and live without any commitment to a deity beyond man. Freud argues:

■ **We say to ourselves, it would indeed be very nice if there were a God, who was both creator of the world and a benevolent providence, if there were a moral world order and a future life, but at the same time it is very odd that this is all just as we should wish it ourselves.[16]**

Marx applied Feuerbach's arguments on political science, and argued that man, "looked for the superman in the fantastic reality of heaven and found nothing there but the reflexion of himself."[17] Karl Marx (1818–1883) is undoubtedly one of the most influential figures of modern time. His grandfather was a Jewish rabbi, and when Marx was six years old his father joined the

Lutheran Church. Marx went to Berlin to study philosophy and came under the influence of a liberal theological lecturer, Bruno Bauer, who was promoting the view that the Gospels are not reliable historically but are simply man's imaginative ideas and desires. Jesus of Nazareth was nothing more than a mythological figure invented by the religious mind. The *Encyclopaedia Britannica* notes:

■ **Marx enrolled in a course of lectures given by Bauer on the prophet Isaiah. Bauer taught that a new social catastrophe "more tremendous" than that of the advent of Christianity was in the making. The Young Hegelians began moving rapidly towards atheism and also talked vaguely of political action.**[18]

Thinking Feuerbach had spoken the last word on religion, Marx uncritically accepted his critique on religion and moved passionately into politics to solve the plight of man. Believing religion is the enemy of man, Marx argues:

■ **Man makes religion, religion does not make man. Religion is indeed man's self-consciousness and self-awareness as long as he has not found his feet in the universe. But man is not an abstract being, squatting outside the world. Man is the world of men, the State, and society. This State, this society, produce religion which is an inverted world consciousness, because they are an inverted world.... Religious suffering is at the same time an expression of real suffering and a protest against real suffering. Religion is the sigh of the oppressed creature, the sentiment of a heartless world, and the soul of soulless conditions. It is the opium of the people. The abolition of religion, as the illusory happiness of men, is a demand for their real happiness.**[19]

Arthur Schopenhauer (1788–1860) rejected all the traditional arguments of God's existence and advocated atheistic pessimism in place of theism. His influence on Friedrich Nietzsche is profound, and the miserable condition of human existence led him to affirm suicide as a possible remedy. It is believed that he slept at night with loaded pistols

beside his bed. He trusted no barber in Germany to shave him with a razor. He lived thirty years in a two-room boarding house and had no companion but a dog. His father committed suicide and his mother died insane.

Auguste Comte (1798–1857), the French atheistic philosopher, rejected God at the age of thirteen and replaced him with the credo, "All is relative." Comte rejected God on cultural and sociological grounds. He grew up in a Catholic home where there was constant conflict and controversy. Unable to bear the pressure, he left his family, declaring himself an atheist. He formulated the philosophy of positivism on the basic assumption of atheism. He attempted to popularize positivism as a substitute for religion. Colin Brown notes:

> ■ **Much to the disgust of thoroughgoing atheists like Nietzsche, Comte proposed a religion of humanity in which God was dethroned and humanity, "the great being," put in his place. He even adapted Catholic worship, priests and sacraments to his secular purposes.**[20]

His writings indicate an absence of theistic understanding and arguments.

Bertrand Russell (1872–1970) is one of the few philosophers who is frequently quoted by atheists. *The Oxford Companion to Philosophy* notes that Russell is, "The most widely read British philosopher of the twentieth century."[21] His writings have influenced a large number of people including the famous musician John Lennon. Although Russell maintained an agnostic position, it would be fair to include him as an atheist on account of a number of his writings and his general attitude to God and religion. Russell, who had a Christian background, rejected God at the age of eighteen after reflecting on the cosmological argument. In his work, *Why I Am Not A Christian*, Russell suggests his reason for rejecting the arguments for God's existence:

He loves you
Yeah, Yeah Yeah
He loves you
Yeah, Yeah
Yeah.

> ■ **I may say that when I was a young man and was debating these questions very seriously in my mind, I for a long time accepted the argument of the First Cause, until one day, at**

the age of eighteen, I read John Stuart Mill's autobiography, and I there found this sentence: "My father taught me that the question, 'Who made me?' cannot be answered, since it immediately suggests the further question, 'Who made God?' " "That very simple sentence showed me, as I still think, the fallacy in the argument of the First Cause.[22]

Jean-Paul Sartre (1905–1981), the French existentialist and the winner of the Nobel prize for literature, advocated an atheism based on Nietzsche's existentialism. According to Sartre the fundamental axiom in philosophy is not essence but existence. "If God exists," argues Sartre, "man cannot be free.

But man is free, therefore God cannot exist. Since God does not exist all things are morally permissible." Hence, man is "an empty bubble on the sea of nothingness."[23] Most of his life Sartre believed that, "All existing things are born for no reason, continue through weakness and die by accident. … It is meaningless that we are born; it is meaningless that we die."[24] Sartre admitted that he once believed in God and later abandoned his religious convictions:

■ **Only once did I have the feeling that He existed. I had been playing with matches and burned a small rug. I was in the process of covering up my crime when suddenly God saw me. I felt His gaze inside my head and on my hands....**

I flew into a rage against so crude an indiscretion, I blasphemed. . . . He never looked at me again.[25]

Among today's atheists Antony G. N. Flew is certainly one of the most passionate. His father was a Methodist minister of religion. His work, *God and Philosophy*, received great attention from both philosophers and theologians. Building on David Hume's skepticism and naturalism, Flew argues for a case which he calls, "Stratonician Presumption."[26] He begins with the presumption of atheism. He explains:

◼ **The presumption of atheism, like the presumption of innocence in the British Common Law, concerns the burden of proof. It is not an assumption that something is the case, it is a thesis about the burden of proof. It is the claim that, if we are rationally to proceed above and behind the universe to some story about the supernatural and transcendent, then we need to have some positive good reason to believe in this story.**[27]

Following the Greek philosopher Strato of Lampascus, Flew insists "that the universe itself is the ultimate explainer."[28] Assuming a naturalistic universe, Flew argues that theism must fit the criterion of naturalism and be open to a strict form of empiricism and falsification.

Flew receives a worthy critique from philosopher Alvin Plantinga in his brilliant work, *God and Other Minds: A Study of the Rational Justification of Belief in God*. Plantinga states:

◼ **The version Flew apparently accepts was recognized very early to be unsatisfactory. As Hempel remarks in a slightly different connection, one must suppose that if a given statement is meaningful, so is its denial. Flew's criterion does not meet this condition: for (as Hempel remarks) although a universal statement like, All crows are black passes the test, its existential denial does not. There is at least one pink unicorn is consistent with any finite and consistent set of observation statements.**[29]

To this list one must add the names of A. J. Ayer, Kai Nielsen, John Mackie, George H. Smith, Wallace T. Matson, Walter Kaufmann, Pierre

Bayle, Albert Camus, and J. N. Findlay. All these men are outspoken apostles of atheism.

III. THE ARGUMENTS OF ATHEISM

Although a large number of atheists accept atheism without reason, a good number of them affirm atheism on the basis of several arguments. These arguments differ one from another, but they are the standard arguments employed by the atheistic apologists:

1. The existence of God is incompatible with the existence of evil (Mackie).[30]
2. God is a projection of man's imagination (Feuerbach).[31]
3. Since God cannot be scientifically demonstrated, God cannot exist (Flew).[32]
4. People believe in God because they are culturally conditioned (Freud).[33]
5. The idea of God is nonsensical like the idea of square-circles (Matson).[34]
6. If God made the world who made God? (Russell).[35]
7. Since there is no evidence of God's existence, God does not exist (Kaufmann).[36]

On the strength of these arguments atheists deny the existence of God. These objections, however, have been adequately answered by a great number of Christian philosophers. We will briefly respond to the above arguments, but for a fuller response please consult the works suggested in the footnote.[37]

1. This objection does not logically deny the existence of God but merely questions or challenges God's character or means of operation. The existence of evil is not incompatible with the existence of God. There is no logical contradiction. In order to make a contradiction the atheist must introduce new premises or assumptions. The atheist presumes a world view because of a prior assumption which he entertains which is, "Evil should not exist with God." This assumption "begs the question." (See Chapter Two.)
2. This objection invented by Feuerbach and popularized by Freud is without substance. The argument is guilty of committing the "genetic fallacy." In the genetic fallacy one seeks to discredit a view by merely going to its

origin. One does not disprove a belief by merely going back and describing how that belief originated. You do not refute a belief by simply dating it or explaining its origin. The psychological objection is not a logical explanation but a logical fallacy.[38]

3. The person who seeks to refute God on the basis of science commits the fallacy of reductionism or scientism. To test God on the basis of science is to use a false criterion. Science is useful in testing a number of phenomena, but to suggest that God must fit the scientific dress is arbitrary and wrongheaded. Science is useful for testing some things but not all things. This objection is also guilty of committing the categorical fallacy, e.g. "Tell me, what is the taste of blue?" The person who argues all things must be tested by science is not able to test the assertion "All things must be tested by science." How does one test love, values, morals, logic, beauty, etc., scientifically?[39]

4. This argument if taken to its logical conclusion would not only refute Christianity but also the atheistic beliefs. The person who advocates this assumption must also be prepared to be judged by this principle. If all beliefs are conditioned, then the unbeliever is also conditioned not to

3

"All existing
things are born
for no reason,
continue
through
weakness and
die by accident.
... It is
meaningless
that we are
born; it is
meaningless
that we die."
Jean-Paul Sartre

believe. This is a two-edged sword which will not only kill your enemy but will also kill you. The atheists cannot claim special privileges and escape philosophical scrutiny. To suggest that only religious people have hang-ups is to propose a false psychology, a questionable sociology, and an unverified scientific theory.

5. This is a straw man argument. The person defines God arbitrarily and subjectively, that God is equivalent to a square circle. Such a move is really in essence building a straw man: in this method you define your opponent's position conveniently in order to shoot him down. To suggest that God is like a square circle is arbitrary. The atheist has no logical or epistemological ground for making this assumption.[40]

6. This objection presupposes that God had a beginning. The argument "Everything has a cause, God is a thing, therefore God must have a cause" is a simple version of a "straw man argument." Here the atheist subjectively and arbitrarily equates God to the order of the created and finite thing. By setting God up on the level of the created, the atheist insists that God must have a cause too. From a logical point of view, "Everything that begins has a cause," but not as the atheists irrationally argue, "Everything must have a cause." Only finite beings and effects need causes; God by definition and essence is not an effect or something made. God is the unmade eternal Creator of the universe. To argue that an unmade being is a contradiction, the atheist must explain how one could maintain the concept of an "uncaused universe." What is sauce for the goose is sauce for the gander.[41]

7. The logical response to this objection is to first examine the nature of evidence – what constitutes evidence. Since there is a great amount of dispute as to what is legitimate evidence, we must first settle the issue of evidence. Since the nature and existence of God is unlike any other issue or category, one must approach God's existence axiomatically. If God is the basic ground of reality, then the issue of God's existence is not on the same plane as the issue of the existence of finite elements like humans and potatoes. For example, take the nature of air: debating the existence of God, in a sense, is like debating the existence of air while breathing. If God is the creator of the universe, then he is the necessary pre-condition for all of reality. If God exists, he is the essential element for all existence. (See Chapter One.)

Christian thinker Alphonse Gratry writes:

■ **The actual theory of atheism … entails at the close of the argument a manifest absurdity; which must be so, since a correct train of reasoning must reduce to an absurdity the hypothesis that there is no God.**[42]

In reality atheists deny not the God of the Bible but an idol of their own imagination.

IV. THE ABSURDITY OF ATHEISM

Is atheism logical? Can one really be an atheist on logical grounds? How does an atheist know with certainty that there is no God? On what ground is atheism believable? What proof is there for atheism? These are questions one must answer if one wishes to be an atheist.

It is fallacious to argue as some atheists such as Gordon Stein, George Smith, Michael Martin, Michael Scriven and Anthony Flew[43] do, insisting on the "presumption of atheism."[44] Philosopher L. Russ Bush explains, "Atheism is like 'innocence' in English law. It is to be presumed until 'guilt' (theism) is proven beyond reasonable doubt."[45] To suggest that the atheist does not have the burden of proof is, in a sense, refusing to play the game but nevertheless insisting on getting the prize at the end of the game. The atheist is in fact begging the question and becoming philosophically self-righteous. Evangelical philosopher William Lane Craig rightly notes, "Atheism is a claim to know something ('There is no God') just as much as theism ('There is a God'). Therefore, it can claim no presumption when the evidence is equal."[46]

Atheism is essentially a religion based on blind faith – it takes greater faith to be an atheist. The atheist by faith believes there is no God and without any evidence believes the universe was uncreated. With no absolutes he believes in morality. Without a foundation he believes in value and without God he believes in life. Atheism is a religion without God, a faith without reason, and a journey without a destiny. An atheist is not a person without beliefs but one who upholds a variety of beliefs. What Mark Twain said equally applies to the atheist, "**It is amazing what a man will believe as long as it is not in the Bible.**" To be an atheist you must accept the impossible, believe the ridiculous, and trust the absurd. From a logical point of view it is impossible to disprove God:

Premise 1. The statement "God does not exist" is a universal negative.

Premise 2. But in principle it is impossible to prove a universal negative.

Conclusion: Therefore atheism is false.

Observe the irrationality of the atheistic premise. The only way for the atheist to be absolutely certain that there is no God is for the atheist to know everything about reality. In order to maintain the premise, "There is no God," the atheist must have total knowledge of all reality. He must know all facts and realities of existence. This would imply that an atheist must have a knowledge which only God could possess. He must possess infinite knowledge throughout time, be everywhere at the same time and be absolutely sure of everything. In reality the atheist must be omniscient, omnipresent, and omnipotent, in which case the atheist must become God in order to prove there is no God. In fact he has to become the very God he is seeking to disprove. But the atheist says there is no God, so how could he argue his position? There is no way by which he could defend his case. Consider the analogy: in order for me to affirm that there is no pin in your room I must examine every space in your room, then conclude there is no pin in your room. It would be meaningless to assert there is no pin in your room when I only have a limited knowledge of your room, therefore the assertion there is no pin in your room cannot be made without total knowledge of your room. Atheism falls into the category of what logicians call "self-refuting statements." J. P. Moreland points out:

■ **When a statement fails to satisfy itself (i.e. to conform to its own criteria of validity or acceptability), it is self-refuting. Such statements are necessarily false. The facts which falsify them are unavoidably given with the statement when it is uttered.**[47]

He provides examples like, "I cannot say a word of English," which is self-refuted when uttered in English. He adds, "The claim, 'There are no truths,' is self-refuting. If it is false, then it is false. But if it is true, then it is false as well, for in that case there would be no truths, including the statement itself."[48] No one knows enough to be an atheist. There is no logical ground for atheism. Atheism is logically impossible. The basis by which the atheist proclaims his faith is empty. He has no foundation, rationality, or epistemology for his denial of God.

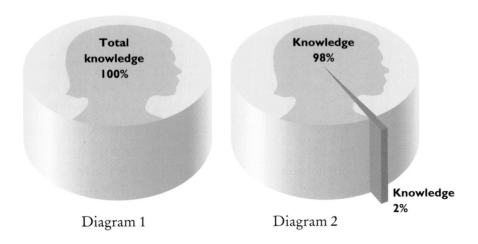

Diagram 1   Diagram 2

The above diagrams illustrate this truth. The first diagram represents total knowledge of reality. It includes everything there is to know, it represents one hundred percent knowledge. The logical question we must ask is, "How much of this knowledge does the atheist possess?" Very little! Einstein said he knew less than half of one percent. Let us be generous and give the atheist two percent of total knowledge. The second diagram represents the knowledge of the atheist in relation to total knowledge of reality. The next logical question: "Is it possible for God to exist outside the knowledge the atheist possesses?" The answer, logically yes! Then how can the atheist say there is no God? He cannot logically say there is no God. Is it any wonder the Bible says, "**The fool says in his heart, 'There is no God'**" (Psalm 14:1 NIV)?

Speaking at a university, I encountered a student who professed to be an atheist and who declared that there was no God. I asked, "Are you absolutely sure there is no God?" "Yes," he replied. Then I remarked, "You have absolute knowledge to be absolutely sure there is no God?" He replied, "No, I don't!" I responded, "Then you are not absolutely sure there is no God?" His response was, "I believe there is no God." Atheism is a belief based on faith. In *What I Believe*, Bertrand Russell, the famous philosopher, admits, "**I do not pretend to be able to prove that there is no God.**"[49] It's not surprising that Nietzsche exclaimed in his work, *The AntiChrist*, "**If one were to prove this God of the Christians to us, we should be even less able to believe in him.**"[50]

An atheist is not one who has no faith. He has no faith in God, but he puts his faith and trust in the belief that there is no God. No one lives in a vacuum. Every person believes in something. The atheist is committed to a set of beliefs. The atheist by faith believes that atheism is true. He offers no evidence for his belief but merely imagines there is no God, because God is outside of his frame of thinking.

The atheist mind-set is adequately illustrated in an analogy employed by the famous scientist Sir Arthur Eddington. He spoke of a fisherman who argued from his experience with a particular net that "No creature of the sea is less than two inches long." The people did not believe it: they affirmed that a great number of sea creatures were shorter than two inches and simply slipped through the holes in his net. But the fisherman was unconvinced. He insisted, "What my net can't catch ain't fish," and went on accusing his opponents of having a pre-scientific, medieval, and metaphysical bias. The atheist commits the same fallacy. He confines God to a particular point of reference and defines him out of existence. The net which the atheist habitually uses is hopelessly deficient – what I cannot see does not exist. Whatever does not fit into my view of reality (naturalism – the reductionistic view which insists that all reality is just matter and excludes the supernatural) is meaningless. His blind faith in naturalism will not allow anything supernatural, transcendent, and metaphysical. It is at this point that the atheist is letting fish slip through his atheistic net.

A clear example of this appeared in the classic debate between Bertrand Russell and Frederick Copleston. Russell, arguing from a naturalistic base, insisted that God was a meaningless proposition outside empirical verification. Copleston gave a fitting response which merits our attention:

■ **The proposition that metaphysical terms are meaningless seems to me to be a proposition based on an assumed philosophy. The dogmatic position behind it seems to be this: What will not go into my machine is non-existent, or it is meaningless.[51]**

The atheist in reality is engaged in explaining and defining God out of existence. Explaining God does not necessarily disprove his existence. The problem is that naturalism is not an adequate net to catch the truth of all realities. It has too many holes in it to hold much truth. Naturalism not only fails to explain the great things of life but desperately fails to explain even the most simple facts of life.

Anyone who rejects the existence of God must believe the following creed:

The Creed of Atheism

1. Matter is eternal.
2. Matter without life created life.
3. Matter without mind created mind.
4. Matter without intelligence created intelligence.
5. Matter without morals created morals.
6. Matter without conscience created conscience.
7. Matter without purpose created purpose and order.

Plato was right, "Atheism is a disease of the soul before it is an error of the mind."[52] Nietzsche boldly declared against his religious background, "But we do not at all want to enter into the kingdom of heaven: we have become men — *so we want the kingdom of earth.*"[53] G. K. Chesterton's dictum has much wisdom, "When people stop believing in God, they do not believe in nothing: they believe almost in anything." Atheism is rationally impossible. In order to be an atheist one must:

1. Prove there is no God.
2. Refute all the evidence for the existence of God.
3. Explain away the reality of Christ.
4. Remove the evidence for the resurrection of Christ.
5. Disprove all the prophecies in the Bible.
6. Demonstrate that the Bible is a fraud.
7. Establish the credibility of atheism.

V. THE AGONY OF ATHEISM

Some time ago they buried an atheist dressed up in a beautiful tuxedo. After a tombstone was placed on his grave, a cynic wrote the following words, "Here lies an atheist all dressed up but nowhere to go." Atheism is a journey without a destiny, a body without a soul, a religion without reason, life without meaning, a faith without hope, and a universe without God.

The truth of atheism is the death of truth. The absence of God logically means the absence of all that

God implies. In Nietzschean terms the death of God means the death of reason, morals, good, value, virtue, and ultimately the Christian view of man. As one college cynic declared, "God is dead, Marx is dead, and I'm not feeling too well myself."

Atheism is existentially unfulfilling. Sigmund Freud concluded, "**The moment a man questions the meaning and value of life, he is sick, since objectively neither has any existence.**"[54] Nietzsche found life unbearable without God and finally went mad. He wrote, "**My life now consists in the wish that it might be otherwise with all things that I comprehend, and that somebody might make my 'truths' appear incredible to me.**"[55] Jean-Paul Sartre admitted that it was distressing that God does not exist because it implies that man tragically stands alone in an empty space and a meaningless universe without a spiritual home. Jackson Pollock struggled with the problem of not being able to live on the basis of atheism. He complained that there was no God and denied any purpose or design in life. He became exhausted by his style of chance painting and committed suicide. Albert Camus was insightful when he wrote, "**To kill God is to become god oneself: it is to realize on this earth the eternal life of which the Gospel speaks.**"[56] Bertrand Russell said, "**I have to read at least one detective book a day to drug myself against the nuclear threat.**"[57]

John Cage advocated an atheistic universe which exists by blind chance and sought to live on the basis of his chance philosophy, but he couldn't live his atheistic chance philosophy when he tried to apply it to his hobby of mushroom picking. He admits, "**I became aware that if I approached mush-**

rooms in the spirit of my chance operations, I would die shortly.... So I decided that I would not approach them in this way."[58] In an important sense atheism proves the existence of God. D. E. Roberts, Professor of Philosophy at New York University, speaking about atheists, suggests, "They offer us the strongest possible argument FOR God that can possibly be conceived."[59]

With great agony the Nobel prize winner Samuel Beckett describes his atheistic condition:

■ **How am I, an a-temporal being imprisoned in time and space, to escape from my imprisonment, when I know that outside space and time lies nothing, and that I, in the ultimate depths of my reality, am nothing also?**[60]

Listen to the agonizing words of Bertrand Russell:

■ **That man is the product of causes which had no provision of the end they were achieving; that his origin, his growth, his hopes and fears, his loves and his beliefs, are but the outcome of accidental collections of atoms; that no fire, no heroism, no intensity of thought and feeling, can preserve an individual life beyond the grave; that all the labour of the ages, all the devotion, all the inspiration, all the noonday brightness of human genius, are destined to extinction in the vast death of the solar system, and that the whole temple of Man's achievement must inevitably be buried beneath the debris of a universe in ruins – all these things, if not quite beyond dispute, are yet so nearly certain, that no philosophy which rejects them can hope to stand. Only within the scaffolding of these truths, only on the firm foundation of unyielding despair, can the soul's habitation henceforth be safely built.**[61]

It would not be off the mark to state an old maxim which touches the core of atheism, "God does not exist because his existence threatens my world view."

Atheism offers no answer to the fundamental metaphysical questions regarding the reality of the universe or the genesis of human personality. The testimony of Robert J. Dean, a scientist, provides a remarkable insight into the position of atheism:

◼ **My father and mother were deeply religious. My brother and I had no time for religion. We thought that religion was all right for old people, but we were scientists and we thought we had found our way through what we were pleased to call scientific methods. Then my brother was killed. My father and mother had resources, and with their resources they could meet that shattering loss. But I had no one. I had no resources at all.**[62]

When his confidence in atheism was shattered, this scientist decided to test the reality of God and found to his satisfaction that God is real. It is more reasonable to believe in God. For the existence of this life is an enigma without the supposition of God's existence.

The brilliant writer and Nobel prize winner for literature, Alexander Solzhenitsyn, came to the right conclusion after observing the consequences of atheism. In a speech before a group of students at Harvard University, Solzhenitsyn insisted:

◼ **If I were asked today to formulate as concisely as possible the main cause of the ruinous revolution that swallowed up some 60 million of our people, I could not put it more accurately than to repeat: "Men have forgotten God; that is why all this has happened."**

CHAPTER 4

If ever God was man or man was God,
Jesus Christ was both.

LORD BYRON

If the life and death of
Socrates are those of a
philosopher, the life and
death of Jesus Christ are
those of a God.

JEAN-JACQUES ROUSSEAU

I tell the Hindus
that their lives will be imperfect
if they do not also study reverently
the teaching of Jesus.

GANDHI

THE CASE FOR THE DEITY OF CHRIST

WHY believe in Jesus Christ?

What makes him so different from Socrates, Buddha, Confucius, and others? Can we be sure of his existence? What evidences support his claim to divinity? Is he relevant to modern man? Why do Christians believe in him?

In an age of conflicting religious claims, no issue challenges the modern mind more than the authenticity of the founder of Christianity. Nearly 2,000 years ago in a province of the Roman Empire there lived a man whose life altered the entire history of the western world. Through the centuries theologians have debated on his origin, skeptics have denounced his existence, and philosophers have wrestled over his teachings. Today he is still the center of discussion, a point for debate, and a source of inspiration to many who follow his teachings. Philip Schaff is on good ground when he states:

■ Jesus of Nazareth, without money and arms, conquered more millions than Alexander, Caesar, Mohammed and Napoleon; without science and learning, He shed more light on things human and divine, than all the philosophers and scholars combined; without the eloquence of the school, He spoke words of life such as were never spoken before, nor since, and produced effects which lie beyond the reach of orator or poet; without writing a single line, He has set more pens in motion and furnished themes for more sermons, orations, discussions, works of art, learned

83

volumes, and sweet songs of praise than the whole army of great men of ancient and modern times. Born in a manger and crucified as a malefactor, He now controls the destinies of the civilized world, and rules a spiritual empire which embraces one-third of the inhabitants of the globe.[1]

Whatever assumption we might entertain about Christ, we cannot dismiss him from the facts of history. We may ignore him, but we cannot avoid him. We may reject him, but we cannot escape him. His name is written across every page of modern history. Every time we write a letter we acknowledge his entrance to our planet. He is indeed a stubborn fact of history. The modern Jewish novelist Sholem Asch affirms, "Jesus Christ is the outstanding personality of all time . . . every act and word of Jesus has value for all of us. He became the Light of the World. Why shouldn't I, a Jew, be proud of that?"[2]

Jesus of Nazareth is one of a kind. There is simply no comparison, as John H. Gerstner delightfully puts it:

■ **To the artist He is the one altogether lovely. To the educator He is the master teacher. To the philosopher He is the wisdom of God. To the lonely He is a brother; to the sorrowful, a comforter; to the bereaved, the resurrection and the life. And to the sinner He is the Lamb of God that taketh away the sin of the world.[3]**

I. THE CERTAINTY OF HIS EXISTENCE

One of the most amazing facts about contemporary skepticism regarding the existence of Christ is that it comes not from experts in ancient history who are trained in historical studies and ancient historiography, but from non-specialists. Recent theories of Christology advocated by the Jesus Seminar people, John Selby Spong, Barbara Thiering, A. N. Wilson, and others, have not succeeded in replacing the historical view. These writers at best are sensational and have a fertile mind for imagination. Their fanciful theories have been adequately refuted by a number of contemporary scholars.[4] Distinguished scholars in ancient history like A. N. Sherwin-White, Sir William Ramsay, B. W. Henderson, F. F. Bruce, C. F. D. Moule, Ethelbert Stauffer, C. H. Dodd, and many others, have accepted without question the historicity of Christ.

The famous writer and agnostic H. G. Wells, in his popular work, *The*

Outline of History, referring to Jesus, affirms, "Here was a man. This part of the tale could not have been invented."[5] Will Durant, an equally famous agnostic and former professor of Philosophy of History at Columbia University, perhaps America's foremost historian, in his article "Caesar and Christ" declares:

> ■ **That a few simple men should in one generation have invented so powerful and appealing a personality, so lofty an ethic, and so inspiring a vision of human brotherhood, would be a miracle far more incredible than any recorded in the gospels.[6]**

Otto Betz points out, "No serious scholar has ventured to postulate the non-historicity of Jesus."[7] F. F. Bruce, who was Rylands professor of Biblical Criticism at the University of Manchester, writes:

> ■ **Some writers may toy with the fancy of a "Christ-myth," but they do not do so on the ground of historical evidence. The historicity of Christ is as axiomatic for an unbiased historian as the historicity of Julius Caesar. It is not historians who propagate the "Christ-myth" theories.[8]**

Theodore Parker's delightful aphorism ought not to escape us, "It takes a Newton to forge a Newton. What man could have fabricated a Jesus? None but a Jesus."[9] Even such an unbelieving writer as James Frazer notes, "The doubts which have been cast on the historical reality of Jesus are, in my judgment, unworthy of serious attention."[10] He concludes, "The origin of a great religious and moral reform is inexplicable without the personal existence of a great reformer."[11]

The case for Christianity depends on the historicity of Jesus Christ. In this sense, Christianity differs from all other religions. Michael Green is right, "Once disprove the historicity of Jesus Christ, and Christianity will collapse like a pack of cards."[12] The conviction of John Stuart Mill is worth noting:

> ■ **It is of no use to say that Christ as exhibited in the gospels is not historical. ... Who among his disciples or among their proselytes was capable of inventing the sayings ascribed to Jesus, or of imagining the life and character revealed in the gospels? Certainly not the fishermen of Galilee, still less the early Christian writers.[13]**

The evidence for the existence of Christ is simply so unbeatable that, if the critics wish to challenge his existence, they would be wise to heed the words of W. H. Fitchett before doing so: "When any one undertakes to prove that Christ did not exist nineteen hundred years ago, he may well be asked to attempt a feat much nearer at hand. Let him prove that He does not exist to-day!"[14] The essence of the Christian message is the entrance of Jesus of Nazareth into space-time history. As British historian Herbert Butterfield rightly points out, "It would be a dangerous error to imagine that the characteristics of an historical religion would be maintained if the Christ of the theologians were divorced from the Jesus of history."[15]

It is on very good ground that Johann Wolfgang Goethe declares:

■ **I esteem the Gospels to be thoroughly genuine, for there shines forth from them the reflected splendour of a sublimity, proceeding from the person of Jesus Christ, and of as Divine a king as was ever manifested upon earth.**[16]

II. THE SECULAR EVIDENCE

Secularists seldom pay serious attention to religious issues, and one should not expect to find an abundance of evidences from secular sources. However, there are adequate evidences from secular writers to establish the historicity of Christ apart from the biblical narratives.

One of the most significant pieces of evidence comes from Pliny the Younger, the governor of Bithynia in Northern Turkey, in the year A.D. 112. In his correspondence to the Emperor Trajan, Pliny makes reference to Christ, "They were in the habit of meeting on a certain fixed day before it was

light, when they sang an anthem to Christ as God, and bound themselves by a solemn oath not to commit any wicked deed..."[17]

A Syrian named Mara Bar-Serapion, in A.D. 70–150, wrote to his son, Serapion, a letter which is preserved in the British Museum. He acknowledges the existence of Jesus. Part of the letter reads, "What advantage did the Jews gain from executing their wise King? It was just after that their kingdom was abolished."[18] Cornelius Tacitus, the famous Roman historian, being governor of Asia Minor in A.D. 112, reveals his knowledge of the existence of Christ, "Christus, from whom they got their name, had been executed by sentence of the procurator Pontius Pilate, when Tiberius was emperor..."[19] The Roman historian Suetonius (A.D. 120) in his book, *The Life of Claudius*, makes an interesting reference to the fact of Christ's existence, "As the Jews were making constant disturbances at the instigation of Chrestus, he expelled them from Rome."[20]

III. THE JEWISH EVIDENCE

The Jewish historian Flavius Josephus, in his famous work, *Antiquities of the Jews* (published A.D. 93), makes several references to familiar figures in the New Testament. They include, among many others, John the Baptist, Pilate, the Herods, Felix, Festus, Annas, Caiaphas, and James "the brother of Jesus." His reference to Christ reads, "And there arose about this time Jesus, a wise man, if indeed we should call him a man: for he was a doer of marvellous deeds, a teacher of men ...."[21] Even if the above passage is questionable, what are we to make of his second reference? "So he (Ananus) assembled a council of judges, and brought before it the brother of Jesus the so-called Christ, whose name was James ...."[22] Professor Ethelbert Stauffer, of the University of Erlangen, in his *Jesus and His Story*, informs, "In A.D. 95 Rabbi Eliezer ben Hyrcanus of Lydda speaks of Jesus' magic arts."[23]

In the Jewish document, *The Talmud*, one could find numerous allusions to Jesus. Rabbi Eliezer said, "Balaam looked forth and saw that there was a man, born of a woman, who would rise up and seek to make himself God, and cause the whole world to go astray."[24] Jewish writer Joseph Klausner, in his work *Jesus of Nazareth*, provides ample Jewish evidence for the historicity of Christ.

We must agree with F. F. Bruce, "Whatever else may be thought of the evidence from early Jewish and Gentile writers ... it does at least establish, for those who refuse the witness of Christian writings, the historical character of Jesus Himself."[25]

IV. THE CREDIBILITY OF HIS CLAIMS

What makes Christ so different from all other men of history? Why is he so special to the Christian? What is it about him that is unique? Moses did not claim to be God; Paul was horrified when people tried to worship him;

Confucius was confused about the nature of God; Zoroaster was a follower of God, never God; Buddha never identified himself as God; Mohammed did not claim to be Allah but, Jesus Christ did – Jesus claimed to be God in the flesh. This very fact set him apart from every other man. C. S. Lewis

points out, with his usual brilliance, the radical differences between the claims of Christ and the claims of other religious leaders:

- **There is no half-way house and there is no parallel in other religions. If you had gone to Buddha and asked him, "Are you the son of Bramah?" he would have said, "My son, you are still in the vale of illusion." If you had gone to Socrates and asked, "Are you Zeus?" he would have laughed at you. If you had gone to Mohammed and asked, "Are you Allah?" he would first have rent his clothes and then cut your head off. If you had asked Confucius, "Are you Heaven?" I think he would have probably replied, "Remarks which are not in accordance with nature are in bad taste."[26]**

John H. Gerstner writes:

- **It is true that Bronson Alcott once said to a friend, "Today I feel that I could say, as Christ did, I and the Father are one." "Yes," the other replied, "but the difference is this: Christ got the world to believe him."[27]**

Most of the world's religious founders stressed the importance of their teachings, but Christ focused on himself. He made it clear that man's eternal destiny depends on how we regard him: "I told you that you would die in your sins; if you do not believe that I am the one I claim to be, you will indeed die in your sins" (John 8:24 NIV).

The claims of Christ are truly staggering. Very few leaders have made the kinds of claims Christ has made. His claims have dazzled many of his disciples, muddled many religious leaders, and puzzled a great number of scholars. Henry J. Heydt said:

■ **No founder of any religion has dared to claim for himself one fraction of the assertions made by the Lord Jesus Christ about himself. No religion has claimed for its founder what Christianity has claimed for the Lord Jesus Christ. No founder of any religion has been as highly acclaimed by those of other faiths as has the Lord Jesus Christ.[28]**

His claim to divinity sets him apart from every other claim. Jesus claimed the highest title which only God could have:

JESUS CLAIMED:
1. To forgive sin Matthew 9:1–8.
2. To judge the world John 5:27, 30.
3. To give eternal life John 3:16.
4. To be sinless John 8:46.
5. To be the object of faith John 8:24.
6. To answer prayer John 14:13.
7. To be worthy of worship Matthew 14:33.
8. To be the Truth John 14:6.
9. To have all authority Matthew 28:18.
10. To be one in essence with God John 10:30.

In Matthew 26:63 and John 5:25 the phrase "Son of God" is used, but this does not mean that he is less than deity, as some wrongly believe. Theologian J. Oliver Buswell, in his *A Systematic Theology of the Christian Religion*, points out:

■ **In Jewish usage the term "son of . . ." did not generally imply any subordination, but rather equality and identity of nature. Thus Bar Kokba, who led the Jewish revolt A.D. 132–135 in the reign of Hadrian, was called by a name which means "Son of the Star." It is supposed that he took this name to identify himself as the very Star predicted in**

4

"I esteem the Gospels to be thoroughly genuine, for there shines forth from them the reflected splendour of a sublimity, proceeding from the person of Jesus Christ, and of as Divine a king as was ever manifested upon earth."

Johann Wolfgang Goethe

Numbers 24:17. The name Son of Consolation (Acts 4:36 [KJV]) doubtless means, "The Consoler." "Sons of Thunder" (Mark 3:17) probably means "Thunderous Men." "Son of Man," especially as applied to Christ in Daniel 7:13 and constantly in the New Testament, essentially means "The Representative Man." Thus for Christ to say, "I am the Son of God" (John 10:36) was understood by His contemporaries as identifying Himself as God, equal with the Father, in an unqualified sense.²⁹

John R. W. Stott writes:

■ **So close was His connection with God that He equated a man's attitude to Himself with the man's attitude to God. Thus, to know Him was to know God (John 8:19; 14:7). To see Him was to see God (12:45; 14:9). To believe in Him was to believe in God (12:44; 14:1). To receive Him was to receive God (Mark 9:37). To hate Him was to hate God (John 15:23). And to honor Him was to honor God (5:23).³⁰**

Any sensible person facing these claims is led to only four possible conclusions:

1. Jesus claimed to be God but knew he was not: Therefore he was a liar.
2. Jesus thought he was God but he was not: Therefore he was a lunatic.
3. Jesus never claimed to be God but his followers created the idea: Therefore it is a legend.
4. Jesus claimed to be God because he was God: Therefore he is Lord.

A serious reflection on the above propositions will lead any rational person to the fourth position. The ministry of Christ and his teaching goes against the nature of a lunatic. For example, take his Sermon on the Mount which is universally regarded as the highest ideal for living, even by non-Christian writers.

Even those who deny his divinity assert that Christ was a great moral teacher. Even a famous atheist like Lord Boothby admits, "I believe the teachings of Jesus are the best that have been offered to mankind."³¹ The overwhelming testimony of the world is that Jesus of Nazareth was a perfect man. When it comes to principles of morality the world knows of no principles superior to those of Christ. The famous historian W. E. H. Lecky, in his significant work, *History of European Morals from Augustus to*

Charlemagne, comments on the life of Christ, "That the simple record of three short years of active life has done more to regenerate and to soften mankind, than all the disquisitions of philosophers and than all the exhortations of moralists."[32] The fact is, how could he be a great moral teacher if he was lying about the nature of his true being? If Jesus is wrong in the crucial area of his own life, he could hardly be a great moral teacher! Professor A. M. Hunter of Aberdeen University makes an important point:

■ **No mortal man makes such a claim, or we know him to be mad. We are driven back on the words of wise old "Rabbi" Duncan: "Christ either deceived mankind by conscious fraud, or He was Himself deluded, or He was divine. There is no getting out of this trilemma."[33]**

Jean-Jacques Rousseau asks, "Can the Person whose history the Gospels relate be himself a man? . . . Yes, if the life and death of Socrates are those of a philosopher, the life and death of Jesus Christ are those of a God."[34] If we accept Jesus as a perfect man, we must also accept him as God. But why should we? John H. Gerstner rightly answers:

■ **Because the perfect man says He is God. And if He is not God, then neither can He be a perfect man. We despise Father Divine as a man for claiming to be God, which we know he is not. If Jesus Christ is not God, we must despise Him also, for He claims far more clearly than Father Divine that He is God. We must, therefore, either worship Christ as God or despise or pity Him as a man.[35]**

As we observe the life of Christ, we see no evidence of mental illness or psychological disturbance. The facts will not permit us to conclude that he was schizophrenic or paranoid. C. S. Lewis sums up the real point of the argument:

FOR GOODNESS SAKE! YOU'RE NOT A POACHED EGG — YOU'RE A BOILED EGG

■ **A man who was merely a man and said the sort of things Jesus said would not be a great moral teacher. He would either be a lunatic – on a level with the man who says he is a poached egg – or else he would be the Devil of Hell. You must make your choice. Either this man was, and is, the Son of God: or else a madman or something worse. You can shut Him up for a fool, you can spit at Him and kill Him as a**

93

demon; or you can fall at His feet and call Him Lord and God.[36]

V. THE CREDENTIALS OF HIS DEITY

Anyone can claim to be God, but what proof do we have to back up that claim? Christ did not just make empty claims about his divinity but proved them with adequate evidence. Luke writes, "He showed himself to these men and gave many convincing proofs that he was alive" (Acts 1:3). The credential of Christ is his resurrection from the dead. It is the resurrection event that separates Jesus Christ from any other individual. In this important event we see Christ's unique demonstration of divinity. Clark Pinnock's remarks are worth noting, "If there is a God and if he wanted us to know that his authority was vested in the invitation of the gospel, he could scarcely have done a more appropriate thing than he has done in raising Christ."[37]

Along the same line the brilliant American philosopher Richard L. Purtill argues:

■ **If I claim to have authority in a certain organization, strong evidence of my authority would be an ability to suspend the rules or make exceptions to usual procedures. You might meditate on the problem of how a God who never interfered with the working of the universe could establish a message from Himself as authoritative.**[38]

The Scripture is very plain, "If Christ has not been raised, our preaching is useless and so is your faith" (1 Corinthians 15:14 NIV). Paul E. Little rightly affirms:

■ **Jesus' supreme credential to authenticate his claim to deity was his resurrection from the dead. Five times in the course of his life he predicted he would die. He also predicted how he would die and that three days later he would rise from the dead and appear to his disciples.**[39]

The apostle Paul, writing to the Romans, says, "Who through the Spirit of holiness was declared with power to be the Son of God by his resurrection from the dead: Jesus Christ our Lord" (Romans 1:4 NIV). Without the resurrection there would not be a Christianity – Christianity stands or falls with the resurrection, and this single factor makes Christianity remarkably one of a kind. The brilliant scholar James Orr perceptively notes:

■ **No single example can be produced of belief in the resurrection of an historical personage such as Jesus was: none at least on which anything was ever founded. ... The Christian Resurrection is thus a fact without historical analogy.[40]**

B. B. Warfield asserts, "Christ Himself deliberately staked His whole claim to the credit of men upon His resurrection. When asked for a sign He pointed to this sign as His single and sufficient credential."[41] The critics of Christianity are fighting a losing battle. Christianity cannot be refuted, simply for one reason: we cannot explain away the resurrection. It is this fact which brought life and courage to the disappointed and disillusioned disciples. It is because

of this event that Christianity spread across the Roman Empire and continues to influence our present world.

What evidences do we have for the resurrection? How can we be sure that Christ rose from the dead? What evidence supports the resurrection?

Fact 1. Christ died on the cross.
Fact 2. Christ was buried.
Fact 3. Christ's disciples were discouraged.
Fact 4. Christ's tomb was empty.
Fact 5. Christ appeared to the disciples.
Fact 6. The disciples were transformed.
Fact 7. The disciples proclaimed the resurrection.

The evidence for the resurrection is in the three indisputable facts: The empty tomb, the resurrection appearances, and the origin of Christianity. These provide solid evidence that Christ rose from the dead. If these facts are true and the alternative theories against the resurrection are inadequate, then we must accept the resurrection as a historical fact.

We agree with Richard Riss, "It is certainly the case that it takes more faith to believe, against the evidence, that the resurrection did not occur, than it does to believe that it has occurred."[42] Dr. Thomas Arnold, the author of the famous three-volume *History of Rome* and professor of Modern History at Oxford, a scholar who was acquainted with historical evidence and an authority capable of weighing facts from fiction, after studying the evidence for Christ's resurrection, states, "I know of no one fact in the history of mankind which is proved by better and fuller evidence of every sort, to the understanding of a fair inquirer, than the great sign which God has given us that Christ died and rose again from the dead."[43]

C. S. Lewis' poignant analysis should move us:

■ **If the thing happened, it was the central event in the history of the Earth – the very thing that the whole story has been about. Since it happened only once, it is by Hume's standards infinitely improbable. But then the whole history of the Earth has also happened only once; is it therefore incredible? Hence the difficulty, which weighs upon Christian and atheist alike, of estimating the probability of the Incarnation. It is like asking whether the**

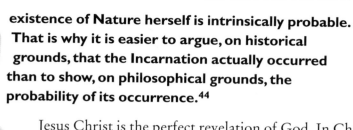

existence of Nature herself is intrinsically probable. That is why it is easier to argue, on historical grounds, that the Incarnation actually occurred than to show, on philosophical grounds, the probability of its occurrence.[44]

Jesus Christ is the perfect revelation of God. In Christ we see what God is like. He is our clue to the existence of God, the meaning of life and the hope of our destiny. Philip Schaff, the Yale scholar, is right in stating, "Standing on this rock, I feel safe against all the attacks of infidelity. The person of Christ is to me the greatest and surest of all facts; as certain as my own personal existence."[45]

That God should reveal himself in our space and time is too great for our small hearts. This unique event is too wonderful to be true. It is simply incredible that the God of the universe should take such a humble step to communicate his infinite love to mankind. This is the meaning and the message of Christ. "No one has ever seen God, but God the One and Only, who is at the Father's side, has made him known" (John 1:18 NIV).

There is a book
worth all other books in the world.

PATRICK HENRY

A man has deprived himself of
the best there is in the world who
has deprived himself of a
knowledge of the Bible.

WOODROW WILSON

The existence of the Bible,
as a book for the people, is the
greatest benefit which the human
race has ever experienced. Every
attempt to belittle it is a crime
against humanity.

IMMANUEL KANT

IS THE BIBLE THE WORD OF GOD?

5

Is the Bible really the Word of God? Can we be sure that God has spoken through the Bible? How do we know that the Bible is really true? What makes the Bible more authoritative than the Qur'an and Bhagavad Gita? And how do we go about demonstrating its authenticity? These are pressing questions which confront every thinking person. Here is a challenge which every Christian will face, and a challenge which cannot be ignored. It demands an answer.

In the age of science and technology, modern man cannot escape facing ultimate questions regarding existence, truth, authority, meaning, and destiny. Remarkably, the Bible astonishes the modern mind as does no other book. No other book has influenced man and history as has the Bible; its influence is reflected in the works of artists, poets, statesmen, musicians, sculptors, and scientists. From Shakespeare to Browning and Longfellow the Bible shines through. No other ancient book has been copied and recopied over such a long period of time as much as this book. No other book has gone through the process of variation and yet come through as remarkably accurate as the Bible.

The Bible is unlike any other book in the world. Its history is striking, its message is impeccable, its influence is incomparable, its unity is amazing, and its accuracy is remarkable. How do we explain its uniqueness? Is it a collusion or just a coincidence? It is far too complex to accept those options! Speaking about the Bible, Jean-Jacques Rousseau, a French philosopher, declares, "I must confess to you that the majesty of the scriptures astonishes me … if it had been the invention of man, the invention would have been greater than the greatest heroes."[1] Consider the following:

1. The world's first printed book was a Bible: Gutenberg's Bible.
2. The most expensive book in the world is a Bible: Gutenberg's Bible.
3. One of the most expensive manuscripts in the world is the Sinaiticus manuscript of the Bible.
4. The longest telegram in history is the Revised Version of the New Testament sent from New York to Chicago.
5. The largest first edition of any book in history was a Bible: the R.S.V., 1,000,000 copies.

The Bible was written over a period of 1,500 years by more than forty different authors from different walks of life, and over forty generations: Moses, a political leader; Amos, a herdsman; Solomon, a king; Luke, a physician; Matthew, a tax collector; Peter, a fisherman.

It was written on three continents: Asia, Africa, and Europe. It was written in three languages: Hebrew, Aramaic, and Greek. It was written in different places: Moses in the wilderness; Daniel in a palace; Jeremiah in a dungeon; Paul in a Roman prison; Luke while travelling. It was written at different times: David wrote in times of war; Solomon in times of peace. It was written in different moods: some authors wrote from the heights of joy and others in the depths of sorrow.

The Holy Bible is an amazing book. When we consider its uniqueness, it is indeed a book of wonder; there is no other book which can come near it. Dr. Bernard Ramm pertinently observes:

■ **A thousand times over, the death knell of the Bible has been sounded, the funeral procession formed, the inscription cut on the tombstone, and the committal read. But somehow the corpse never stays put.**

No other book has been so chopped, knifed, sifted, scrutinized, and vilified. What book on philosophy or religion or psychology or belles lettres of classical or modern times has been subject to such a mass attack as the Bible? with such venom and skepticism? with such thoroughness and erudition? upon every chapter, line and tenet?

The Bible is still loved by millions, read by millions, and studied by millions.... It still remains the most published and most read book in the world of literature.[2]

The Bible touches on a variety of controversial topics, such as the problem of man, the destiny of the universe, the nature of happiness, the way of redemption, the hope of the world, etc. In spite of its diversity there is one story, one theme, one solution, and one plan of redemption for mankind. Don Stewart, after examining the uniqueness of the Bible, remarks:

■ **How can this be explained? By the fact that there is only one author behind all of the books of the Bible: God Himself. The unity of the Bible is only one unique feature that separates it from all other books ever written.[3]**

Werner Keller, a former skeptic, had a hard time believing the Bible to be God's Word, but finally he came to believe it. In his book, *The Bible as History*, he concludes:

■ **In view of the overwhelming mass of authentic and well-attested evidence now available, as I thought of the sceptical criticism which from the eighteenth century**

···· *IT HAS POSSIBILITIES.*

THE BIBLE

PUBLISHERS

onward would fain have demolished the Bible altogether, there kept hammering in my brain this one sentence: "The Bible is right after all."[4]

The case for the Bible depends not merely on its uniqueness but on five solid grounds which establish beyond reasonable doubt that the Bible is the Word of God.

I. REASON DEMANDS IT

It is reasonable to believe that the Bible is a divine revelation. Reason can lead the open-minded skeptic to the conclusion that the Bible is from God. As we approach the Bible we are logically limited to two alternatives. Either the Bible is a worthless fraud or the Bible is in truth the Word of God. It is either the words of man or a revelation from God. There is no other alternative. Every person has a basis of authority which becomes a ground for operations of his or her thinking and living. In some cases the basis of authority is highly complex, for it is made up of several things, and too often people are ignorant of the fact that they have such a thing as a basis of authority. But everyone, without exception, has one.

Through the centuries, man's greatest quest has always been to know, "Why am I here?" "Where did I come from?" and, "Where am I going?"

Only an infinite God can answer our greatest questions. Modern man is desperately struggling in darkness for the answers to the questions of life. Without divine revelation, man's search for truth is a hopeless quest. Without a message from God, man's life is a fathomless riddle, man's existence a dark mystery, and death a wicked joke. In his book, *Modern Man In Search of a Soul*, psychoanalyst Carl Jung correctly points out, "Human thought cannot conceive any system of final truth that can give a patient what he needs in order to live."[5] Without a divine revelation one can never understand the lessons of the past, the meaning of the present, and the direction for the future. Logically speaking, if the Bible is not from God, we cannot rely on its content nor derive hope or comfort from its promises.

Man needs a divine revelation, but only God can provide such a revelation. Nature is inadequate to act as a guide for the existence of man. It takes an infinite being to provide infinite truth. We need absolute truth to be absolutely sure, but man is finite and limited, hence he cannot act as an authority on, nor possibly ascertain any notion of, ultimate truth. If there is no absolute truth or ultimate authority to appeal to, we have no obligation to do anything!

Only God is in a position to speak with absolute knowledge to the needs of man. R. C. Sproul wisely asserts, "Only God can provide us with an eternal perspective and speak to us with absolute and final authority."[6] This sentiment is eloquently argued by no less an authority than Ludwig Wittgenstein, perhaps the most respected philosopher of the twentieth century, in his remarkable work, *Tractatus Logico-Philosophicus*, "If there is any value that does have value, it must lie outside the whole sphere of what happens and is the case. For all that happens and is the case is accidental." He further adds, "It is clear that ethics cannot be put into words. Ethics is transcendental."[7] This apt statement evokes the following comment from John W. Montgomery:

> ■ **The plain consequence is that the only possible answer to modern man's quest for the ultimate meaning of history and for an absolute ethical standard would have to lie in a revelation from outside the world. If such a revelation does not exist, man will of logical (not merely practical) necessity remain forever bound to his cultural relativities, forever ignorant of life's meaning. But if such a revelation should exist, it would explode the world – turn it, as men said the early Christians did, upside down (Acts 17:6 [KJV]).[8]**

Where can we turn to solve the question of truth, the meaning of life and the problem of man? With all his wisdom man has never been able to provide an absolute answer to the question of his existence nor offer a meaning to his life, nor chart a course through the fog of unhappiness, uncertainties, and untold misery of human existence. As Sproul so adequately states:

■ **The world's best geographer cannot show us the way to God, and the world's best psychiatrist cannot give us a final answer to the problem of our guilt. There are matters contained in Holy Writ that "unveil" for us that which is not exposed to the natural course of human investigation.[9]**

From a logical point of view, if man is to know the truth of God, it is essential that God reveal his truth to man. Since only God has absolute truth and all things are possible with God, it is logically conceivable that God could communicate his truth to man. If God exists, he can speak to man; since man needs God's truth, it would be reasonable for God to provide man with his truth. God has met man's need in every other dimension of existence; what would prevent God from meeting our ultimate need? There is nothing in reason which denies the possibility for a divine revelation.

In fact, man cannot know God's will without God's revelation. God, being infinite in power, is able to communicate with man, and, since revelation is both possible and necessary, it is therefore reasonable that God should give man a revelation. There is nothing in reason which denies the possibility for such a revelation.

II. HISTORY VERIFIES IT

If the Bible is really the Word of God, we would expect to find it historically reliable. Unlike all other writings of world religions, the Bible is historically verifiable. Historian after historian has accepted the trustworthiness of the Scriptures. The reliability of biblical documents is well argued in such standard texts as James Martin's, *The Reliability of the Gospel*; F. F. Bruce's, *The New Testament Documents: Are They Reliable?* and, *The Defense of the Gospel in the New Testament*. Dr. Clark Pinnock, professor of Interpretation at McMasters University in Canada, rightly observes:

- **There exists no document from the ancient world witnessed by so excellent a set of textual and historical testimonies, and offering so superb an array of historical data on which an intelligent decision may be made. An honest man cannot dismiss a source of this kind. Skepticism regarding the historical credentials of Christianity is based upon an irrational bias.[10]**

The wonder of the Bible stands not simply on its ethical teachings but on its historical facts. The Bible contains many facts of history. In Luke, chapter three, verse one, we have fifteen historical references all in one verse:

- **In the fifteenth year (one) of the reign of Tiberius Caesar (two)—when Pontius Pilate (three) was governor (four) of Judea (five), Herod (six) tetrarch (seven) of Galilee (eight), his brother Philip (nine) tetrarch (ten) of Iturea (eleven) and Traconitis, (twelve) and Lysanias (thirteen) tetrarch (fourteen) of Abilene (fifteen) [NIV].**

Any classical historian could check out the historical accuracy of the above references. This implies that the Bible is historically verifiable. Historian Will Durant, in his momentous work, *The Story of Civilization*, makes comments on the gospel writers that should be noted:

- **They record many incidents that mere inventors would have concealed – the competition of the apostles for high places in the Kingdom, their flight after Jesus' arrest, Peter's denial, the failure of Christ to work miracles in Galilee, the references of some auditors to his possible insanity … no one reading these scenes can doubt the reality of the figure behind them.[11]**

H. G. Wells, the famous agnostic historian, acknowledged the Gospels as historical documents in his popular work, *The Outline of History*:

■ **Almost our only sources of information about the personality of Jesus are derived from the four gospels, all of which were certainly in existence a few decades after his death. Here is a man. This part of the tale could not have been invented.**[12]

The Bible is historically reliable; it provides facts for our faith. Modern man need not speculate aimlessly on the nature of Christ's existence. The Bible offers us some hard facts about life. "Christianity," writes Richard Riss, "claims to be based upon something more than mere speculation, and if its claims are true, the implications are overwhelming."[13]

The historical reality of the Bible is one of a kind. No other religious book can match its reliability or authenticity. G. B. Hardy makes this point with great eloquence in his delightful book, *Countdown*:

■ **When you consider the great writings of the Egyptians, the Babylonians, the Greeks and the Romans, how they are saturated with mythology, superstition, and fantasy ... replete with scientific blunders, surely it is impossible the Bible could escape without error. Still it stands without a single proven error after thirty-four centuries of scholarship.**[14]

If the Bible is God's Word, it must not contradict God's world. If God spoke through the Bible, one would expect the Bible to speak accurately about the facts and events in history. Josephus, the Jewish historian and contemporary of Christ, provided powerful evidence for the reliability of the New Testament. His work, *Antiquities*, offers abundant references, facts, figures, and characters found in the New Testament. Dr. F. F. Bruce, who was Rylands Professor of Biblical Criticism and Exegesis in the University of Manchester, summed up the historical evidence:

■ **Here, in the pages of Josephus, we meet many figures who are well known to us from the New Testament: the colorful family of the Herods; the Roman emperors Augustus, Tiberius, Claudius, and Nero; Quirinius, the governor of**

Syria; Pilate, Felix, and Festus, the procurators of Judea; the high-priestly families – Annas, Caiaphas, Ananias, and the rest; the Pharisees and Sadducees; and so on.[15]

In the light of the overwhelming evidence we fully concur with Francis Piper, "What the church lacks in our day is not a reliable text of the Bible, but the faith in the sufficiently reliable text."[16] The brilliant New Testament scholar at Princeton, J. Gresham Machen, concludes:

■ **We know that the gospel story is true partly because of the early date of the documents in which it appears, the evidence as to their authorship, the internal evidence of their truth, the impossibility of explaining them as being based upon deception or upon myth.**[17]

THE ANCIENT MANUSCRIPTS

AUTHOR	DATE WRITTEN	EARLIEST COPY	TIME SPAN	COPIES
Plato	400 B.C.	A.D. 900	1300 years	7
Caesar	100 B.C.	A.D. 900	1000 years	10
Aristotle	300 B.C.	A.D. 1100	1400 years	5
Tacitus	A.D. 100	A.D. 1100	1000 years	20
Herodotus	400 B.C.	A.D. 900	1300 years	8
Thucydides	400 B.C.	A.D. 900	1300 years	8
Livy	A.D. 30	A.D. 900	900 years	20
New Testament	A.D. 100	A.D. 200	100 years	5300

III. ARCHAEOLOGY SUPPORTS IT

The accuracy of the Bible is abundantly confirmed by the science of archaeology. Dr. James H. Jauncey states, "Archaeology is the science which investigates the ruins of ancient civilizations with a view to reconstructing their history and finding out the truth with regard to their customs and ways of living."[18] The significance of archaeology to the Bible is twofold: Firstly, it provides objective evidence for the accuracy of biblical accounts. Secondly, it offers greater insight and factual information to biblical narrative. The Bible makes innumerable references to historical events and characters. These references include dates, customs, people, behavior, places, and cities. Archaeological research done in Bible lands has amazingly confirmed the reliability and historicity of the Scriptures in so many areas. Every part of the Bible that could be checked by archaeology now provides the most positive proofs for the

5

"Through the wealth of data uncovered by historical and archaeological research, we are able to measure the Bible's historical accuracy. In every case where its claims can be thus tested, the Bible proves to be accurate and reliable."
Jack Cottrell

The gates of ancient Nineveh during modern reconstruction after excavation accuracy of the Bible. Archaeologist Dr. Joseph Free, in his book, *Archaeology and Bible History*, writes, "Archaeology has confirmed countless passages which have been rejected by critics as unhistorical or contradictory to known facts."[19] We concur with the judgment of Jack Cottrell, who contends:

> ■ **Through the wealth of data uncovered by historical and archaeological research, we are able to measure the Bible's historical accuracy. In every case where its claims can be thus tested, the Bible proves to be accurate and reliable.[20]**

During the nineteenth century, when liberal theology was at its height, the Bible was commonly treated as a book of legends, myths and fiction. Many of its characters and events were rejected as unhistorical. Many liberal critics argued that the Hittite race never existed and Abraham was just a mythological figure. The critics strongly charged that Moses could not have written the first books of the Bible since writing was not invented then. The Gospel of John was supposed to have been written by a second-century individual who had no contact with the events reported. The unbelieving critics insisted that the book of Acts was a legendary account with no historical basis and not written by Luke but composed by an unknown author living in the second century.

Today, archaeology has refuted the skepticism of the critics and confirmed the reliability of biblical history. No eminent scholar would share the liberal view of the nineteenth century critics. The liberal, critical view has no historical basis and cannot be maintained intellectually on the basis of archaeology. It has been wisely said that every time the spade goes into the ground, a liberal theory is buried. The world-renowned archaeologist and palaeographer Dr. William F. Albright, of Harvard University, rightly points out:

- **The excessive skepticism shown toward the Bible by important historical schools of the eighteenth and nineteenth centuries, certain phases of which still appear periodically, has been progressively discredited.[21]**

Jauncey fully agreed with the above conviction when he declared, "In almost every area where the Bible was criticized on subjective or theorizing grounds, it has already been vindicated on this objective basis."[22] Using the Bible as a guide, the renowned Jewish archaeologist Nelson Glueck has discovered more than a thousand ancient sites in Trans-Jordan and 500 more in the Negev. In writing a review on Keller's book, *The Bible as History*, in the *New York Times*, Professor Glueck states:

- **The reviewer has spent many years in biblical archaeology, and, in company with his colleagues, has made discoveries confirming in outline or in detail historical statements in the Bible. He is prepared to go further and say that no archaeological discovery has ever been made that contradicts or controverts historical statements in Scripture.[23]**

Archaeology has confirmed the culture and customs of Abraham's day; it has brought to light the great Hittite empire previously unknown to historians. It has proven the accuracy of Luke's writings at every point where it is possible to verify. The classic works of A. T. Robertson, *Luke the Historian in the Light of Historical Research*, and of Sir William M. Ramsay, *St. Paul the Traveller and the Roman Citizen*, record these findings.

Ramsay as a young professor set out to uncover contradictions between the biblical records and actual archaeological findings. But after years of doing archaeological research in Asia Minor and Greece, Ramsay was forced to reverse his opinion. His research confirmed the reliability of the Bible, and he became a firm believer in the authority of the Scriptures – so convincing was the evidence that he became a Christian. Ramsay describes his conviction:

- **I take the view that Luke's history is unsurpassed in regard to his trustworthiness. ... You may press the words of Luke** in a degree beyond any other historian's and they stand the keenest scrutiny and the hardest treatment.[24]

Norman L. Geisler writes, "It has been largely due to the archaeological efforts of the late great Sir William Ramsay that the critical views of New Testament history have been overthrown and its historicity established."[25] Millar Burrows of Yale University, writing on archaeology, points out:

■ **On the whole, however, archaeological work has unquestionably strengthened confidence in the reliability of the Scriptural record. More than one archaeologist has found his respect for the Bible increased by the experience of excavation in Palestine.[26]**

Donald J. Wiseman, the director of the British Museum and a specialist in the field of archaeology, informs us:

■ **The geography of Bible lands and visible remains of antiquity were gradually recorded until today more than 25,000 sites within this region and dating to Old Testament times, in their broadest sense, have been located.[27]**

It is amazing how an ancient book can receive such overwhelming support from the science of archaeology. The logic of Dr. Jauncey cannot be faulted, "If the Bible has been shown to be truthful in these obscure details, it is very unlikely that any part of it is the work of a forger."[28]

If all the lines of evidence demonstrate the reliability of the Bible, then

the Bible's own claims to being God's inspired Word should be taken seriously. Sir Frederic G. Kenyon, the famous British classical scholar, who was principal librarian and the director of the British Museum for twenty-one years, summed up the evidence:

> **The Christian can take the whole Bible in his hand and say without fear or hesitation that he holds in it the true Word of God, handed down without essential loss from generation to generation throughout the centuries.**[29]

IV. PROPHECY PROVES IT

One of the most powerful evidences for the divine origin of the Bible is the remarkable number of fulfilled prophecies found in it. The Bible contains numerous predictions of events which were actually fulfilled. The successful fulfillment of these prophecies is valid proof of divine direction and supernatural assistance. God alone knows the future, and he is the only being who has the ability to predict future events. Bernard Ramm adds:

> **Prophecy is thus by its nature a manifestation of the supernatural light of God. The reason for this is derived from an inspection of the powers of the human mind. We can probe into the past by the means of the science of historiography. We can probe into space by virtue of the telescope and the ancilliary sciences developed around astronomy ... but there is no knowledge of the future that compares in certainty and accuracy with our knowledge of past time and outer space.**[30]

The Bible itself makes the fulfillment of prophecy the test for its own validity, and thus the reputation of the Bible stands on prophecy. It has been estimated that prophecy constitutes 34 percent of the entire content of the Bible. God himself agrees to let his statements stand or fall by the test of prophecy, and he invites others to do the same:

> **"Present your case," the LORD says. "Bring forward your strong *arguments*," the King of Jacob says. Let them bring forth and declare to us what is going to take place; as for the former *events*, declare what they *were*, that we may consider them, and know their outcome; or announce to us what is coming. Declare the things that are going to come afterward, that we may know that**

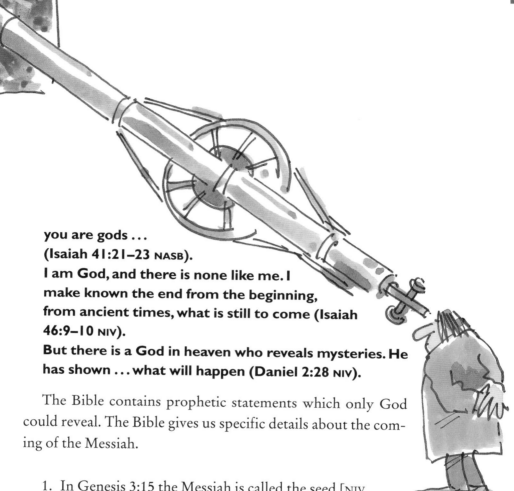

you are gods ...
(Isaiah 41:21–23 NASB).
I am God, and there is none like me. I
make known the end from the beginning,
from ancient times, what is still to come (Isaiah
46:9–10 NIV).
But there is a God in heaven who reveals mysteries. He
has shown ... what will happen (Daniel 2:28 NIV).

The Bible contains prophetic statements which only God could reveal. The Bible gives us specific details about the coming of the Messiah.

1. In Genesis 3:15 the Messiah is called the seed [NIV margin] of the woman; the Messiah will be born into a human family.
2. In Genesis 22:18; Galatians 3:16 the Messiah will be of the lineage of Abraham.
3. In Genesis 49:9, 10 the Messiah will come out of the tribe of Judah.
4. In 1 Chronicles 1:24–27 the Messiah will be born of the lineage of Shem.
5. In Isaiah 11:1, 2, 10 the Messiah will come out of the lineage of Jesse.
6. In Isaiah 7:14 the Messiah will be born of a virgin.
7. In Isaiah 9:6, 7 and 16:5 the Messiah will be the Son of David.
8. In Micah 5:2 the Messiah will be born in Bethlehem.
9. In Psalm 22:14–18 the Messiah will be crucified.
10. In Psalm 16:9–11 the Messiah will be resurrected.

After his resurrection, Christ spoke to his disciples: "This is what I told you while I was still with you: Everything must be fulfilled that is written about me in the Law of Moses, the Prophets and the Psalms" (Luke 24:44 NIV). We agree with G. B. Hardy:

■ **Only the supernatural mind can have prior knowledge to the natural mind. If then the Bible has foreknowledge, historical and scientific, beyond the permutation of chance … it truly then bears the fingerprint of God.[31]**

V. CHRIST CONFIRMED IT

One good reason why any one should believe the Bible to be God's Word is the testimony of Jesus Christ. Professor A. Rendle Short correctly argues, "The most serious reason for regarding the Bible as the Word of God is because of the respect in which it was held by Jesus Christ."[32] Kenneth Kantzer represented the opinions of many scholars when he wrote, "Christians hold the Bible to be the Word of God (and inerrant) because they are convinced that Jesus, the Lord of the church, believed it and taught His disciples to believe it."[33] On the same note, the British writer John W. Wenham, in his very popular work, *Christ and the Bible*, rightly points out, "To Christ the Bible is true, authoritative, inspired, to him the God of the Bible is the living God, and the teaching of the Bible is the teaching of the living God. To Him what Scripture says, God says."[34] Jesus Christ accepted the Bible as the infallible Word of God. Clark Pinnock is right, "The Bible is not infallible because it says so – but because He says so. There is no more reliable witness to the nature of Scripture than the one who died and rose to be our Savior."[35] Jesus believed that God had spoken in his written revelation, therefore Scripture is God's Word (Matthew 5:18; 19:4; John 10:34; cf. Acts 4:25; 28:25; Hebrews 10:15). Theologian John H. Gerstner correctly observes:

■ **The evidence that Christ did regard the Old Testament Scriptures as inspired is so persuasive that it is seldom contested today even by those who themselves do not accept this inspiration but think that Jesus was mistaken, a victim of the "errors" of his day.[36]**

Along the same line, the brilliant Old Testament scholar Edward J. Young affirms, "Not only did Jesus Christ look upon the Old Testament as forming an organic whole but also he believed that both as a unit and in its several parts it was finally and absolutely authoritative."[37]

For Christ, the Bible is the Word of God. In fact, he used the phrase, "The Word of God," when he referred to certain Old Testament passages. When dealing with the Pharisees, Jesus charged them with replacing the commandment of God with their own tradition, hence they were guilty of "invalidating the word of God" (Mark 7:13 NASB). When he was debating with them about his claim to deity, he appealed to the Scriptures as final and fully authoritative and therefore "the Scripture cannot be broken" (John 10:35 NASB). Christ's frequent and continued appeal to the Scriptures indicates his high view of Scripture.

In the same line, Professor F. F. Bruce, in his excellent work, *The Books and the Parchments*, notes:

■ **In many points He condemned the Jewish tradition, but not with respect to the canonicity of Scriptures. His complaint, indeed, was that by other traditions they had invalidated in practice the Word of God recorded in canonical Scripture.[38]**

It is a fact of history that Christ accepted the Scriptures as God's Word. "But," the critics argue, "why should anyone accept the authority of Jesus?" "If we could accept the words of Jesus, why not accept the authority of Mohammed or Buddha or even Karl Marx? What makes Jesus so special?" This is an important challenge for which we have an excellent reply.

At the early part of our discussion, the author affirmed that the Scripture is reliable material, a fact accepted by leading historians. Its reliability is further supported by the findings of archaeology. Hence, one could logically affirm that the Scriptures are historically reliable. We could argue that the Scriptures, which are reliable, provide information about Jesus Christ who claimed to be God and proved his claims by rising from the dead. Only God has the power of resurrection; Jesus had the power of resurrection, therefore Jesus is God. Whatever God says is true. Jesus who is God says the Bible is God's Word, therefore the Bible is God's Word.

If all religions lead to God,
how come most of them, having been
given a thousand years at least,
haven't yet arrived?

GORDON BAILEY

I believe in Christianity
as I believe that the sun has risen
not only because I see it but because
by it I see everything else.

C. S. LEWIS

CHRISTIANITY AND COMPARATIVE RELIGION

6

WE live in an age of pluralism. Non-Christian religions are emerging in every sector of our society. There is much truth to the old African saying, "He who never visits thinks mother is the only cook." If we visit other countries, watch television, and read the newspapers, we cannot avoid confronting other religions. The western world is no longer monolithic but pluralistic. Gone are those days when Christianity was looked upon as the only religion for the West. R. D. Clements, in his popular book, *God and the Gurus*, writes, "It is quite likely that the whole of Western culture may become increasingly influenced by Eastern ideas."[1] Today, Christians not only face the need of proclaiming the Good News of Jesus Christ, but they also confront the gigantic task of demonstrating the uniqueness of Christianity in the midst of a plurality of religions.

DO ALL RELIGIONS LEAD TO GOD?

One basic assumption of the modern mind is that all religions are both fundamentally the same and superficially different. Those who advocate this view affirm that it does not matter which religion we belong to as long as we believe some sort of something. Mahatma Gandhi declared, "My position is that all the great religions are fundamentally equal." Rama Krishna asserts, "Truth is one; sages call it by various names."[2] This present conviction was

117

strongly held by Symmachus in his classic debate with St. Ambrose when he said, "The heart of so great a mystery cannot be reached by following one road only." "All religions lead to God; they are basically the same and no religion can be wrong," argues the modern religious relativist. Gordon Bailey is right, "If all religions lead to God, how come most of them, having been given a thousand years at least, haven't yet arrived?"[3]

On the surface it appears very loving and tolerant to affirm that all religions are fundamentally equal, but in reality this view leads to the death of religion. We must tolerate the views of others and respect their right to hold their views, but we have no right, in the name of tolerance, to declare that mutually contradictory views are equally true. R. C. Sproul observes, "We must note the difference between equal toleration under the law and equal validity according to truth."[4] The kind of religious tolerance which refuses to pronounce any religion true and others false misses the very truth of religion. Truth is by definition very narrow, and by its very essence is intolerant of error. He who says all religions are the same knows very little about religion. If all religions are the same, what are the fundamentals or the elements that unify all religions as being the same?

In the light of conflicting religious claims, one could either ignore the obvious contradictions among religions, which is a nice way to kill all religions, or consider the major contradictions as non-essentials. Such an approach will bring peace and tolerance, but peace at what price? We may achieve peace, but we will miss the truth. If truth is what matters ultimately, then we cannot ignore conflicting truth-claims. H. P. Owen points out:

■ So far as the transcendental truth claims of religion are concerned the question of objective truth remains. Thus divine reality cannot be both personal and impersonal. Also it cannot be validly interpreted both in theistic and monistic terms. To look at it from the human side, our final bliss cannot consist both in the attainment of Nirvana and in eternal fellowship with a personal God of love.[5]

Love, sincerity, honesty, and faith cannot be the basis for all religions. Hitler sincerely believed in what he was doing – but he was sincerely wrong! A Hindu mother may very lovingly offer her child as a sacrifice to the goddess Kali, but her love will not alter the tragedy. One may have faith that the ten dollars in the pocket is a thousand dollars, but all the faith will not change the fact. Faith must be based on fact; sincerity and love must be grounded in truth. Just because we worship some god doesn't mean that we worship the true God, as Brian Maiden correctly notes, "It is not enough to worship God; we must worship the God who really is. Otherwise we are not really worshipping God at all."[6] We must be certain that what we believe is true and have good evidence that our belief is worthy of our ultimate commitment. Dr. Vernon Grounds was not off the mark when he wrote:

■ **Unless a religion squares with the facts of history and human experience; and unless it agrees with the truth of God which is the underlying reality of all things, that religion, however sincere its followers may be, is not good enough.[7]**

It is not arrogant or unkind to tell the truth lovingly. In reality, those who condone false religion as true are cruel to those who follow a mistaken path. The most loving thing to do to a person on a wrong train is not admire his sincerity and say, "It doesn't matter what you believe, all trains

"YOU ARE ON THE WRONG TRAIN, BUT HAVE A NICE DAY ANYWAY"

6 "To maintain that all religions are paths leading to the same goal, as is so frequently done today, is to maintain something that is not true. Not only on the dogmatic, but also on the mystical plane, too, there is no agreement. It is then only too true that the basic principles of Eastern and Western, which in practice means Indian and Semitic, thought are, I will not say irreconcilably opposed; they are simply not starting from the same premises. "

Professor Zaehner, Hindu scholar

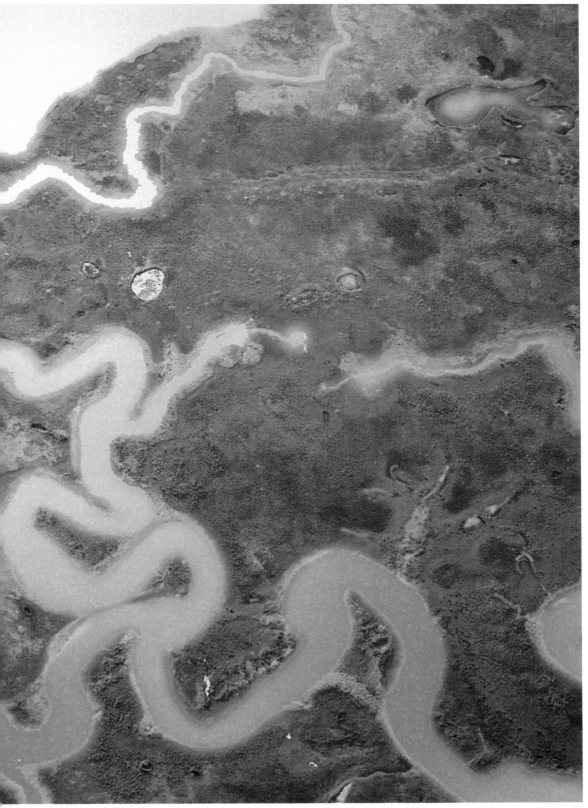

lead to the same place, have a pleasant trip!" Such an action denies the very essence of love and compassion. When a person is on a wrong train, the most loving thing we can do is to share the truth kindly and show him where to find the right one. As Michael Green suggests:

> ■ **It is not that Christians are narrow-minded or uncharitable about other faiths. But if Jesus is indeed, as the resurrection asserts, God himself come to our rescue, then to reject him, or even to neglect him, is ultimate folly.**[8]

All religions differ in their view of who and what God is. Religions make contrary claims. All religions cannot be equally true when they all contradict one another. Opposing convictions cannot both be true. If all religions contradict one another, there are only two logical choices: either they are all false, or there is only one true religion. If there is one true God, then there must be one true way to reach him. If God has communicated to man in Scripture as to how we should please him, then to choose other ways is to deny God's truth and ignore his revelation. Honesty should move us to reflect, in the light of our sin and rebellion, not why there is only one way to God, but why there should be a way at all! Professor Zaehner, the leading Hindu scholar, incisively notes:

> ■ **To maintain that all religions are paths leading to the same goal, as is so frequently done today, is to maintain something that is not true. Not only on the dogmatic, but also on the mystical plane, too, there is no agreement. It is then only too true that the basic principles of Eastern and Western, which in practice means Indian and Semitic, thought are, I will not say irreconcilably opposed; they are simply not starting from the same premises. The only common ground is that the function of religion is to provide release; there is no agreement at all as to what it is that man must be released from. The great religions are talking at cross purposes.**[9]

IS HINDUISM A VIABLE BELIEF SYSTEM?

Hinduism is one of the oldest religions in the world. It dates back to 3000 B.C., and its historical origin is untraceable. It involves a variety of beliefs and practices, and it has been rightly said that Hinduism is more a culture than a creed. According to one Indian, it is a museum of beliefs, a medley of rites, or a mere map, a geographical expression. The word *Hindu* is Persian for "Indian." The Hindu scholar K. M. Sen asserts, "The religious beliefs of different schools of Hindu thought vary and their religious practices also differ ... indeed Hinduism is a great storehouse of all kinds of religious experiments."[10] No less an authority than Radhakrishnan, one of the world's most respected Hindus, in defending Hinduism, declares:

■ **While it gives absolute liberty in the world of thought, it enjoins a strict code of practice. The theist, the sceptic and the agnostic may all be Hindus if they accept the Hindu system of culture and life ... what counts is conduct, not belief.**[11]

In one sense Hinduism is the mother of all eastern thinking. Popular Hinduism has as many as 330 million gods. In the West the question is,

"Does God exist?" but in the East the question is, "Which god to worship?"

What major convictions influence the lives of millions of Hindus? Christopher E. Storrs rightly points out:

■ **The One-without-a-second, the sole Reality; the mirage of this world; the ceaseless wandering from birth to birth; the iron law of Karma which fixes present and future status; Release or Moksha – salvation from an endless cycle in Nirvana.**[12]

Central to Hinduism is the concept "Brahman;" the impersonal, the ultimate reality, the supreme soul of the universe which is beyond all human 123 description. Brahman is one without a second. There is nothing but the one. All reality is one: God is all and all is God. The Hindu affirms, "Truly this whole world is Brahma. In calmness let man worship It as that from which he came forth, as that into which he will be dissolved, as that in which he breathes."[13] Rabindranath Tagore insists:

> **According to some interpretations of the Vedanta doctrine Brahman is the absolute Truth, the impersonal It, in which there can be no distinction of this and that, the good and the evil, the beautiful and its opposite, having no other quality except its ineffable blissfulness in the eternal solitude of its consciousness utterly devoid of all things and all thoughts.[14]**

The Hindu philosopher Shankara asserts, "Brahman alone is real, the phenomenal world is unreal, or mere illusion."[15] As Jack C. Winslow aptly observes:

> **Brahma is conceived as beyond all attributes, including moral attributes. Brahma is neither holy nor unholy, loving nor unloving. Thus the moral challenge contained for the Jew and the Christian in the divine command, "Be ye holy, for I am holy" is lacking in Hinduism … morality belongs to the world of maya, not to the world of ultimate reality.[16]**

Sri Ramakrishna, admired by many as one of the greatest philosophers of nineteenth-century Hinduism, illustrates adequately the Hindu view of ultimate reality which resides within the seeker. In a popular parable he states:

> **A man woke up at midnight and wanted to have a smoke. Needing a light, he went to his neighbour's house and knocked on the door. When the neighbour asked what his midnight visitor wanted, he replied, "I wish to smoke. Can you give me a light?" To which the neighbour answered, "Bah! What's the matter with you? Here you have taken all this trouble to come over here, to say nothing of wakening me, to get a light, when in your own hand you hold a lighted lantern!"**

"Likewise," continues Sri Ramakrishna with the moral, "What a man wants is already within him; but he still wanders here and there in search of it."[17]

The Hindu quest for reality is adequately expressed in the following:

> **Why dost thou go to the forest in search of God? He lives in all, is yet ever distinct: he abides with thee too. As fragrance dwells in a flower, or reflection in a mirror, so**

does God dwell inside everything; seek him therefore in the heart.[18]

Mahatma Gandhi proposed the Hindu world view remarkably well when he said:

◼ **To me God is Truth and Love, God is Ethics and morality, God is fearlessness. God is the source of light and life, and yet he is above and beyond all these. God is conscience. He is even the atheism of the atheist. He transcends speech and reason. He is a personal God to those who need his personal presence. He is embodied to those who need his touch. … He is all things to all men.**[19]

In Hinduism God is not separate from man, God is man. God is the one reality and man has no individual existence outside the reality of God. God is the reality both manifest and unmanifest, transcendent and imminent, infinite and finite, formed and formless, time and timeless, the one beyond all definition and distinction, above our classification of subjective and objective.

The Hindu concept of God is foreign to Christianity. For the rational mind the concept of a pantheistic God raises a number of logical difficulties.[20] The pantheist may suggest that God is beyond reason and continue to affirm the view, but such a leap of faith provides no comfort or hope to a seeking mind. If everything is God, then in reality nothing is God. By calling the universe God we do not change one single fact of reality, rather we commit the intellectual sin of word-magic, where something supposedly receives new life by our giving it a new name. But a rose by a different name is still a rose.

If everything is God, then God is both good and evil. If God is both good and evil, there is no difference between loving or killing someone. Where all is divine, all is good. The Hindu idea of God provides no basis for religious experience. If only God exists, then there are no creatures to experience God, and love is totally impossible in this context, for an impersonal God cannot love man. Ian Barbour states the fundamental difference between Hinduism and Christianity on the subject of selfhood when he points out that for Hindus, "It is the self as such which is the problem, and man should escape the self by detachment from all desires and emotions, or by absorption in divine." But for Christians, he states, "Self-centeredness rather than selfhood itself is the problem, and love toward God and man is the true fulfilment of individuality."[21] Ultimately, the Hindu belief system is very inadequate; to tell a man earnestly seeking God that he is God, is like telling a beggar that he is food! Christopher E. Storrs says:

■ **Hinduism stands poles apart from the faith of the Hebrew prophets with their clear-cut certainty of truth and falsehood, and with their inspired intolerance of false belief or make-believe.[22]**

In essence Hinduism is man's attempt to reach the Transcendent with the brilliance of his wisdom and virtue. It is a remarkable compliment to human achievement. The reality is, man may ask the question, but only God is big enough to give us the answer.

Hinduism offers no cleansing power from guilt and sins. As the common saying goes: "I came to Allahabad; I washed, but my sins came away with me."[23]

HINDUISM vs. CHRISTIANITY

HINDUISM			CHRISTIANITY
Pantheism	◄ METAPHYSICS	►	Theism
Impersonal	◄ GOD	►	Personal
Subjective	◄ TRUTH	►	Objective
Divine	◄ MAN	►	Sinner
Relative	◄ ETHICS	►	Absolute
Self-effort	◄ SALVATION	►	Grace
Ignorance	◄ SIN	►	Rebellion

DOES BUDDHISM ANSWER THE PROBLEM OF LIFE?

There are some 600 million Buddhists around the world. Buddhism was founded in India by Siddhartha Gautama a little more than 500 years before Christ, and during the course of many years, it spread to various parts of Asia. In one sense Buddhism is a Hindu heresy. Buddhism is largely divided into two main groups: the Buddhism that was introduced to China, Japan, and Korea is generally called *Mahayana Buddhism*, meaning the "Great Vehicle," but the Buddhism of Sri Lanka, Burma, Cambodia, Laos, and Thailand is called *Theravada Buddhism*, meaning the "Lesser Vehicle." Various sects and schools have risen from the two main groups. Buddha developed his teachings in the context of Hinduism, seeking to provide a better solution to the problem of human suffering. The Buddhist scholar Shoyu Hanayama notes, "The universal and fundamental doctrines of Buddhism were naturally expounded by Sakyamuni, the founder of Buddhism, but they were not invented by Sakyamuni."[24]

In his book, *The Path of Buddha*, Kenneth W. Morgan suggests, "In Buddhism, there is no such thing as belief in a Supreme Being, a creator of the universe, the reality of an immortal soul, a personal Savior."[25] According to Ninian Smart, the leading scholar in comparative religion, Buddhism is "Mysticism without God."[26] Equally renowned for his contribution to comparative religion, H. D. Lewis from London University asserts that Buddha dismissed "all speculation about other ultimate questions as a useless and even misleading diversion of energy."[27] Buddha taught the "Four Noble Truths" and the "Eight-fold Path" to achieve the ultimate. He never spoke about God or ways to approach him. In the light of this, Buddhism is a philosophy of life rather than a philosophy of God.

THE FOUR NOBLE TRUTHS
1. The Fact of Suffering
2. The Cause of Suffering
3. The Cessation of Suffering
4. The Path to Cessation of Suffering

THE EIGHT-FOLD PATH
1. Right views (right understanding of the Buddha's teachings)
2. Right consideration (of the truth)
3. Right words (which are true)
4. Right conduct (in everyday life)
5. Right way of life (in society)
6. Right efforts (to attain the enlightenment)
7. Right mind (right use of the intellect)
8. Right meditation (to enter Buddhahood)

The desire of every Buddhist is to be free from the problems of life; to be free from pain and suffering. As their saying goes, "As the water of the sea tastes of salt, so all life tastes of suffering. To live is to suffer." Their goal is to develop a detachment from life. Hanayama declares, "The existence of the Self or Ego, which is believed in many religions to exist permanently and apart from one's body, is completely denied in Buddhism."[28] D. T. Suzuki reminds us, "To think that there is the self is the start of all errors and evils. Ignorance is at the root of all things that go wrong."[29]

Buddha taught that desire is the root of all evil. To exist is to suffer and the answer to suffering is Nirvana (annihilation) which is achievable by successive reincarnation. Hence Buddhism insists, "Those who love a hundred have a hundred woes. Those who love ten have ten woes. Those who love one have one woe. Those who love none have no woes." The goal of life is to reach the stage of desirelessness. When we cease to desire we have overcome the burden of life. How one is supposed to be desireless without desiring that quality is a problem few have any time to answer.

According to Buddhism, God is beyond any description, hence it would be proper to include Buddhism in the category of agnosticism. The leading Buddhist scholar, Christmas Humphreys, adequately states:

> ■ **The Buddhist teaching on God, in the sense of an ultimate Reality, is neither agnostic, as is sometimes claimed, nor vague, but clear and logical. Whatever Reality may be, it is beyond the conception of the finite intellect; it follows that attempts at description are misleading, unprofitable, and a waste of time. For these good reasons the Buddha maintained about Reality "a noble silence." If there is a Causeless Cause of all Causes, an Ultimate Reality, a Boundless Light, an Eternal Noumenon behind phenomena, it must clearly be infinite, unlimited, unconditioned and without attributes. We, on the other hand, are clearly finite, and limited and conditioned by, and in a sense composed of, innumerable attributes. It follows that we can neither define, describe, nor usefully discuss the nature of THAT which is beyond the comprehension of our finite consciousness. It may be indicated by negatives and described indirectly by analogy and symbols, but otherwise it must ever remain in its truest sense unknown and unexpressed, as being to us in our present state unknowable.[30]**

Though Buddha was profoundly moved by human suffering, he did not offer a solution to alleviate human suffering. His ethos was not to take the physical reality seriously. Reality according to Buddha is not the external "What" but rather the internal "How." He did not regard himself as divine, nor did he offer any help except his teaching. According to Buddha, "Man is born alone, lives alone and dies alone, and it is he alone who can blaze the way which leads him to Nirvana." *The Buddha Annual of Ceylon* says, "Buddhism is that religion which without starting with a God, leads men to a stage where God's help is not necessary." There is neither God nor a Savior to help man from the problem of life: man must save himself. A Buddhist monk in prayer was once asked by a Christian what he was doing. The Buddhist replied, "I am praying to nobody for nothing." G. K. Chesterton rightly notes, "We may call Buddhism a faith; though to us it seems more like a doubt."[31] The idea of the cross is foreign to the Buddhist. G. Parrinder speaks of a Buddhist who said, "I cannot help thinking of the gap that lies deep between Christianity and Buddhism. The crucified Christ is a terrible sight and I cannot help associating it with the sadistic impulse of a psychically affected brain."[32]

Despite its popularity and simplicity, Buddhism seriously fails to meet the basic problems of life. Alan Watts, the popular Buddhist writer, aptly describes the Buddhist answer, "The solution for us is not solution, but only solution via dissolution."[33] There is a profound difference between the serene and passionless Buddha of Buddhism and the tortured Christ on the cross of Christianity. As philosopher Alfred North Whitehead observes, "Buddha gave his doctrine; Christ gave His life." Man cannot solve his own problem, for there is no human solution to the human problem. However good the Eightfold Path may be, no human self-improvement projects are good enough to make a person perfect before a holy God. George Carey is right, "There is a world of difference between the passive and serene figure of Buddha and the active, suffering figure of Christ."[34] According to G. K. Chesterton, "It was fitting that the Buddha be pictured with his eyes closed; there is nothing important to see."

BUDDHISM vs. CHRISTIANITY

BUDDHISM			CHRISTIANITY
Monism	◄ Metaphysics ►		Dualism
Agnostic	◄ God ►		Theistic
Mystical	◄ Faith ►		Historical
Self-Effort	◄ Redemption ►		Divine Assistance
Detachment	◄ Life ►		Involvement
Enlightenment	◄ Spirituality ►		Regeneration
Reincarnation	◄ Destiny ►		Resurrection

DOES ISLAM OFFER A RELIABLE REVELATION?

Islam is the second largest religion in the world. The word *Islam* in Arabic means "surrender," hence a Muslim is one who has surrendered to the sovereign will of Allah (God). It was founded by Mohammed in the early part of the seventh century, and the sayings of Mohammed are compiled in the Muslims' sacred book called the Qur'an. As H. Kraemer points out, in Islam, "The Word did not become flesh: the Word became Book."[35] Every devoted Muslim believes that the Qur'an is the Word of God. The word Qur'an means "The Readings," and the book is comprised of 114 suras, or chapters. It must not be subjected to any form of question or criticism. Beside the Qur'an the Muslim believes the Hadith and Sunna. These are accepted with respect but they are not equal to the Qur'an. In his book, *History of Religion*, the great scholar E. O. James writes:

■ **Islam, in fact, might be counted almost a Christian "heresy" apart from this new direct revelation, supplementing and completing that vouchsafed through Christ and Hebrew prophets, since the Founder got most of his material from late forms of Judaism and Christianity, often curiously distorted and garbled.[36]**

The central teachings of Islam are the "Five Pillars":

1. Confession that, "There is no god but Allah, and Mohammed is his prophet."
2. Praying five times daily facing Mecca.
3. Giving alms to the poor.
4. Fasting during the month of Ramadan.
5. One pilgrimage to Mecca during a lifetime if possible.

In the world's religions we have man's answer to man's problem, but in Christianity we have God's answers to man's problems. What man has long hoped for religiously through the centuries has taken place in Christ. The infinite has become finite, the abstract concrete, the invisible visible; God became man. This position should not be regarded as narrow-minded exclusivism but as an invitation to share the joy of Christ, as George Carey so aptly describes, "**The supreme gift we bring to others, not arrogantly nor with pride, is that in Jesus our Lord we find the final and complete answer to man's needs.**"[49]

Christianity answers the questions of history, offers a solution to the problem of sin, removes the burden of guilt, releases from the fear of death, reverses despair into hope, and provides power to live a victorious life with God. Stephen Neill's conclusion is therefore completely logical, "**For the human sickness there is one specific remedy, and this is it. There is no other.**"[50]

In one profound sense all other religions have views, but in Christianity we have news – the Good News that God has done something of eternal value for the salvation of man in Jesus Christ. J. Gresham Machen was right when he wrote:

■ **All the ideas of Christianity might be discovered in some other religion, yet there would be in that other religion no Christianity. For Christianity depends, not upon a complex of ideas, but upon the narration of an event.**[51]

Christianity is unique because Jesus Christ is different from all the leaders of the world. He is not just one bead on the necklace of God or "**one note of the flute that Divinity blows.**"[52] In Jesus Christ we have something unique. The apostle Paul gives us good reasons why Christ cannot be put alongside of Buddha, Mohammed, Confucius, Socrates, and Plato. In his letter to the Philippians Paul writes, "**He . . . became obedient unto death, even death on a cross. Therefore God has highly exalted him and bestowed on him the name which is above every name, that at the name of Jesus every knee should bow, in heaven and on earth and under the earth.**" (2:8–10 RSV)

1. RELIABLE REVELATION

The Christian revelation is unlike all other claims to revelation; the Christian revelation is totally reliable. There is more historical evidence for the reliability of the New Testament than of any ten pieces of classical literature put together. The New Testament is one of the most highly researched books of the ancient world. The earliest copy of the writings of Tacitus, the Roman historian, is about a thousand years from the time of the original. A thousand years separate the writing of Caesar's *Gallic War* from the date of the oldest manuscripts, and we have only ten copies. Thirteen hundred years separate the writings of Plato from the written date. The earliest writings of Aristotle which we possess date back fourteen hundred years from the original, but when we come to the New Testament, the gap between the original copies and the existing copies is 30, 100, and 200 years. F. F. Bruce, formerly Rylands Professor of Biblical Criticism at the University of Manchester, writes:

■ **The evidence for our New Testament writings is ever so much greater than the evidence for many writings of classical authors, the authenticity of which no-one dreams of questioning.**[53]

If anyone rejects the reliability of the New Testament, then on the same ground he or she must be prepared to reject all the documents for ancient and classical history. The agnostic historian, H. G. Wells, agrees that the Gospels existed in the first century. He says, "Information about the personality of Jesus is derived from the four gospels, all of which were certainly in existence a few decades after his death."[54] Sir Frederic Kenyon, former director and principal librarian of the British Museum, concluded shortly before his death, "Both the authenticity and the general integrity of the books of the New Testament may be regarded as finally established."[55]

2. RESURRECTED REDEEMER

The Christian faith is based on an historical event – the resurrection. All other major world religions are based on a philosophical or theological system, but Christianity is founded on a space-time event. There is one event in the life of Christ that separates him from every person that ever lived in the history of the world – the resurrection. There is absolutely nothing in any philosophy or religion that compares with what is found in Jesus Christ. G. B. Hardy states it eloquently:

■ **There are but two essential requirements:**
   1. Has any one cheated death and proved it?
   2. Is it available to me? Here is the complete record:
      Confucius' tomb – occupied
      Buddha's tomb – occupied

**Mohammed's tomb – occupied
Jesus' tomb – EMPTY.
Argue as you will ... THERE IS NO POINT IN
FOLLOWING A LOSER.[56]**

The fact that all the founders of the world's religions could not conquer their own death is good evidence that they do not represent the truth. Jesus Christ demonstrates that he is the truth by dying and rising from the grave. If Jesus Christ defeated death, which is man's greatest enemy, then he is the greatest authority on truth and he alone has the right to speak on all the

greatest questions of life, God, and death. Philosopher H. D. Lewis rightly summed it up, "He came in complete human form to meet a universal need in a way that is adequate for all times and places and is without parallel or substitute."[57]

There is more historical evidence for the resurrection of Jesus Christ than there is for the fact that Napoleon was defeated at the battle of Waterloo or that Julius Caesar was a Roman emperor. No theory has ever been produced which could logically refute the reality of the resurrection while adequately considering all the available evidence. The Cambridge scholar Bishop Westcott, writing on the resurrection, states:

■ **Indeed, taking all the evidence together, it is not too much to say that there is no single historic incident better or more variously supported than the resurrection of Christ.**[58]

3. RESOURCEFUL RELATIONSHIP

Christianity is not merely a religion but is a relationship. The Christian faith provides a right relationship between man and God through Jesus Christ. In all the world's other major religions, man tries to work his way to God, but in Christianity God reaches out to save man. In other religions man seeks to redeem himself by his own effort, but in Christianity God redeems man from his sin and failures. God does for man what he cannot do for himself. Religion gives good advice, but Christ offers power and strength to overcome sin and evil.

The story is told that Sadhu Sundar Singh, the great Indian saint, was once traveling in a train with a number of learned Brahmin. "Tell us," they said, "what belief do you have in Christianity that is not found in Hinduism?" Sadhu responded, "I have Christ." They repeated the question and again Sadhu replied, "I have Christ." They asked him for the third time, "What belief do you have in Christianity that is not found in Hinduism?" And again Sadhu replied, "I have Christ." Christianity is Jesus Christ! It

would be fair to affirm that of all the great religious leaders of the world Jesus Christ alone makes the remarkable claim that he is God:

- I and the Father are one (John 10:30 NIV).

  The Son of Man has authority on earth to forgive sins (Mark 2:10 NIV).

  Before Abraham was born, I am (John 8:58 NIV.

  He who does not honor the Son does not honor the Father, who sent him (John 5:23 NIV).

  Behold, I am coming soon! My reward is with me, and I will give to everyone according to what he has done. I am the Alpha and the Omega, the First and the Last, the Beginning and the End (Revelation 22:12, 13 NIV).

Hendrik Kraemer captured the truth when he declared that "Christ is the crisis of all religions."[59] Without him Christianity would be a dead wood. He makes all the difference. Christ is not just a fact to be believed or a topic just for discussion but a living reality to encounter. He is a vital person to know and to love. Only Christianity provides a resource and a solution to the problem of sin. The Bible states, "But God demonstrates his own love for us in this: While we were still sinners, Christ died for us" (Romans 5:8 NIV). The founders of world's religions say, "Do! Do! Do!" but Christ says, "Done! It is finished!" J. N. D. Anderson says:

- This is the unique element in the gospel, which tells us that what we could never do, God has done. We cannot climb up to heaven to discover God, but God has come to earth, in the person of His Son, to reveal Himself to us in the only way we could really understand: in terms of a human life.[60]

This is what makes Christianity so special:

In Jesus Christ:

Our sins are forgiven.
Our guilt is removed.
Our fear of death is destroyed.
Our faith is founded on a personal God.
Our search for truth is satisfied.
Our security and identity are complete.
Our lives are now based on a new hope.

The basic difference between Christianity and the world's religions is this: As a Hindu I was drowning in a large lake and I did not know how to swim.

The religious leaders and gurus came by and gave me lectures on how to swim. Confucius taught, "You should have followed my teaching and then you would never have fallen." Mohammed advised, "Allah wills whatsoever he wills." Buddha came by and said, "It's all an illusion in the mind, change your mind and you will change the problem." Krishna came along and said, "It's your karma that you have fallen into the lake. You deserve it." Then Jesus Christ came. He did not give a lecture or some good advice. He said, "I have come to seek and to save those who are lost," and he came right into the lake and lifted me out of it and changed my life and put a new song in my heart. The song writer captured my sentiment when he wrote, "From sinking sand He lifted me, with tender hands He lifted me. From shades of night to plains of light. Oh, praise His name, He lifted me." I now understand the experience of the psalmist when he said:

■ I waited patiently for the Lord; he turned to me and heard my cry. He lifted me out of the slimy pit, out of the mud and mire; he set my feet on a rock and gave me a firm place to stand. He put a new song in my mouth, a hymn of praise to our God. Many will see and fear and put their trust in the Lord (Psalm 40:1–3NIV).

CHAPTER 7

The gods love
the obscure
and hate the
obvious.
UPANISHADS

The answer to every
problem is that there is
no problem. Let a man
perceive this truth and
then he is without
problems.
MAHARISHI
MAHESH YOGI

ANSWERING THE EASTERN MIND

"THE East is East and West is West and never the twain shall meet,"[1] said Rudyard Kipling a century ago. But today one would be naive to hold such a view. The East and the West are no longer apart but are becoming one. Although the West is influencing the East through its science and technology, the East is making its impact on the West through its religious ideology. Marshall McLuhan observes that the East may be going West in terms of the goal-oriented outer trip, but the West is going East in terms of the inner trip. Theologian Nels F. Ferre adds, "The supernatural, personalistic, classical Christian faith is now being undermined by an ultimately non-dualistic, impersonal or transpersonal faith. The winds are blowing gale-strong out of the Orient."[2]

Gone are those days when the East was looked upon as dark and depraved. Many westerners now admire the East and cherish it as a place to discover spiritual wisdom. Youth, disillusioned with western life-style and humanistic materialism, are turning East with a hope of finding meaning for their existence. Eastern ideas and philosophies are penetrating every sector of western culture. Eastern sects such as the Transcendental Meditation Movement, Divine Light Mission, Hare Krishna Movement, Soka Gakkai, Theosophy, and Zen Buddhism are rapidly increasing and gaining recognition in many areas.

Eastern movements cannot be dismissed as passing fads, nor can they be ignored as obscure cults. Their influence and ideology have serious implications for social, psychological, philosophical, and spiritual life. In the light of these it is imperative that we examine the basic premises of the eastern world view.

I. THE ROOTS OF EASTERN IDEAS

The historical roots of eastern thinking are most intriguing. The climate of opinion in many circles is that the eastern ideas are unique to the East and their basic presuppositions are foreign to the West. These convictions are simply fictional and have no historical ground.

The roots of Hinduism go back to the Aryans who introduced Vedic teaching to the people of India. Prior to the invasion of the Aryans the Indians were animist. This new ideology was similar in essence to that of the Greeks, as Jack C. Winslow points out:

■ **There is, for instance, Varuna, the Greek Ouranos, i.e. Heaven, who in Greek mythology is the father of Zeus, the bright sky. The Vedic equivalent of Zeus is Dyaus, often called Dyauspitar, or Father Dyaus – in Greek, Zeus pater and in Latin, Jupiter.[3]**

The origins of Aryan beliefs are deeply grounded in the mythology and philosophy of the Greeks. Greek philosophers such as Parmenides, Heraclitus, Plotinus, and Pythagoras held to views which are basic to Hinduism and Buddhism. Concepts like pantheism, monism, emanation, and reincarnation are common doctrines among the Greeks. The eastern views of time, history, and existence are identical to those of the Greeks. Os Guinness observes, "Both the Greeks and the Hindus viewed time as cyclical and limitless." He points out, "The Greeks viewed the physical universe as a world of shadow, less true or less real than the transcendent ideal which was beyond knowledge; for the Hindus the physical universe is a world of 'maya,' or illusion."[4]

II. THE BASIC EASTERN BELIEF SYSTEM

Every religion has a belief system, and the East has one which is contrary to Christianity. The test of a belief system must be that it is logically consistent, factually verifiable, and existentially liveable. Any world view which fails the above principles should be rejected. An unwise person may accept the absurd, but a wise person will choose the logical.

Eastern religion functions on the basis of certain theological and philosophical presuppositions. A presupposition is a belief or a conceptual framework of thought accepted as a premise to support one's basic view of life and through which one sees all realities. As philosopher Gordon H. Clark affirms, "Every philosophy must have its first principles."[5] These presuppositions provide a basis for one's ethical, social, and religious life. Behind the practice of Hinduism and Buddhism lie several presuppositions which control the belief systems:

I. REALITY IS ONE

Although eastern religion embraces a wide range of ideas from polytheism to theism, its basic belief system is pantheism or monism. Pantheism affirms that there is only one ultimate reality – God – and everything is part of this reality. We agree with Mark Albrecht, "It may be said with some certainty that no religion or religious philosophy is any better than its conception of God."[6] From Shankara, Vivekenanda, and Radhakrishnan to Maharishi, the main religious system is pantheistic. The *Upanishad* defines ultimate reality as, "That from which these beings are born, that in which born they live, and that into which they enter at their death is Brahman."[7] In the *Bhagavad Gita* Brahman Itself speaks:

■ **All this universe is strung upon me, as rows of gems upon a thread. I am the taste in water, I am the light in moon and sun, sound in the ether, manhood in men. The pure scent in earth am I, and the light in fire; the life in all born beings am I, and the mortification of them that mortify the flesh. I am the understanding of them that understand, the splendour of the splendid.[8]**

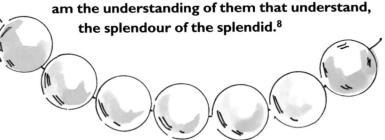

No words could describe Brahman, for it is beyond framework. Brahman is God, being, awareness, and bliss. Sarvapalli Radhakrishnan, known throughout the world as India's greatest philosopher of this century, when asked to define Brahman, remained silent and when pressed to respond, stated, "The Absolute is silence."[9] It is "the divine darkness," and "that of

143

which nothing can be said." Brahman is Atman, the One-without-a-Second. Radhakrishnan argues:

■ He who knows Brahman becomes Brahman. Perfection is a state of mind, not contingent of time or place. ... He who knows himself to be all can have no desire. When the Supreme is seen, the knots of the heart are cut asunder. ... There can be no sorrow or pain or fear when there is no other.[10]

In pantheistic thinking there is no room for any other. The *Upanishad* summed up Brahman as "Thou art that" *Tat tuam asi*:

■ "Place this salt in water and come to me tomorrow morning."
   Svetaketu did as he was commanded, and in the morning his father said to him: "Bring me the salt you put into the water last night."
   Svetaketu looked into the water, but could not find it, for it had dissolved.
   His father then said: "Taste the water from this side. How is it?"
   "It is salt."
   "Taste it from the middle. How is it?"
   "It is salt."
   "Taste it from that side. How is it?"
   "It is salt."
   "Look for the salt again and come again to me."
   The son did so, saying: "I cannot see the salt. I only see the water."
   His father then said: "In the same way, O my son, you cannot see the spirit. But in truth he is there. An invisible and subtle essence is the Spirit of the whole universe. That is Reality. That is Truth. Thou art That!"[11]

Brahman is the only reality, all else is illusionary. As the Hindu philosopher Shankara asserts, "Brahman alone is real, the phenomenal world is unreal, or mere illusion."[12] Where all is divine, everything is one. The logic is, if God is All, there cannot be anything but God. The goal of eastern pantheism is the ontological merging of Atman (self) with Brahman (the Absolute), as consciousness of the self is radically transcended to the oblivion. The true experience of Atman leads to the knowledge of Brahman. The experience of Atman is not objective but subjective, intuitive, and immediate. The pantheist argues that our physical senses often create the impression that we are separate, iso-lated, and individual, but this is due to ignorance. Once we lose the false sense of individuality, we experience pure conscious cosmic unity with Brahman. Commenting on Atman and Brahman the *Upanishads* declare:

> ■ This soul of mine within the heart is smaller than a grain of rice, or a barley-corn, or a mustard-seed, or a grain of millet, or the kernel of a grain of millet; this soul of mine within the heart is greater than the earth, greater than the atmosphere, greater than the sky, greater than the worlds....This soul of mine within the heart, this is Brahman.[13]

As one author puts it, " 'The doer and the Causer to do are one.' 'God tells the thief to go and steal, and at the same time warns the householder against the thief.' "[14] The logic of Stephen Neill is inescapable, "If in fact Brahman and I are

one, there is no one to be offended."[15] The quest of every Hindu is reflected in the prayer of the *Upanishads*:

> ■ Lead me from the unreal to the real. Lead me from darkness to the light. Lead me from death to immortality.[16]

145

The conception that reality is ultimately one is the metaphysical view of not only classical Hinduism but also historical Buddhism. D. T. Suzuki, the leading advocate of Zen Buddhism, affirms:

■ **Simple people conceive that we are to see God as if He stood on that side and we on this. It is not so; God and I are one in the act of my perceiving Him. In this absolute oneness of things, Zen establishes the foundation of its philosophy.[17]**

According to Mahayana Buddhism, reality is beyond any categories of existence:

■ **Suchness (reality) is neither that which is existence nor that which is non-existence; neither that which is at once existence and non-existence; nor that which is not at once existence and non-existence; it is neither that which is unity nor that which is plurality; neither that which is at once unity and plurality, nor that which is not at once unity and plurality.[18]**

Is God the rock, the tree, and energy that emits from them? Are we not insulting God by reducing him to the level of plants and animals? Is there no difference between a painter and his painting, a creator and his creation? Is

pantheism really an intellectual option for modern man? When one seriously reflects on the pantheistic idea that reality is one, it should not take too long to discover the impossibility and the difficulty of such a notion. If reality is ultimately one, then there are no finite individuals. But to assert, "reality is one" in a strictly monistic context would be senseless. If only God exists, who is God talking to? Pantheism is impossible. To affirm, "God exists but I am not," is self-contradictory since one must exist in order to make the statement. The denial of dualism and the affirmation of pantheism is irrational since the pantheist must exist as a separate individual (which refutes pantheism) to make statements on the nature of existence. If pantheism is true, no pantheist should advocate pantheism, since such an activity presupposes the existence of other beings who need to be convinced about pantheism.

The logic of Norman L. Geisler should challenge every pantheist:

■ **When we cross a busy street and see three lanes of traffic coming towards us, should we not even worry about it because it is merely an illusion? Indeed, should we even bother to look for cars when we cross the street, if we, the traffic and the street, do not really exist? If pantheists actually lived out their pantheism consistently, would there be any pantheists left?[19]**

SCREECH · ·

Pantheists teach that man is deceived in thinking of his individual existence. If this be the case, how could the pantheist know that he is not mistaken when he thinks reality is one? If the real is unreal and the obvious is false, how do we know that the pantheists are really telling us the truth? On what basis is the pantheist so sure that he is not mistaken? Do the pantheists possess a special pipeline to reality? If reality is one, relationship and religious experience would be impossible and meaningless. If God alone exists, God and not the pantheist is having the experience. Professor John Warwick Montgomery's insightful analysis of pantheism is worth noting:

■ **Pantheism ... is neither true nor false; it is something much worse, viz., entirely trivial. We had little doubt that the** universe was here anyway; by giving it a new name ("God") we explain nothing. We actually commit the venerable intellectual sin of Word Magic, wherein the naming of something is supposed to give added power either to the thing named or to the semantic magician himself.[20]

Writing on the same issue C. E. M. Joad, former professor of philosophy at London University, in his book, *Guide to Philosophy*, insists:

■ If we assume that Substance in the original definition means simply "all that there is," then it is the conclusion. Such a conclusion is not worth proving. It is, indeed, merely a tautology – that is to say, an asserting of the same thing in two different ways.[21]

The fallacy of pantheism is not only a logical error, but it has serious moral implications. If God is All and All is God, then evil is part of God. "Since the pantheist God," writes Mark Albrecht, "is of one essence with creation and consciousness, God is thus the origin of the imperfection and evil in our world; the foulest deeds and thoughts of humanity literally become attributes of God."[22]

Francis Schaeffer illustrates the serious implication of pantheism:

■ One day I was talking to a group of people in the digs of a young South African in Cambridge. Among others, there was present a young Indian who was of Sikh background but a Hindu by religion. He started to speak strongly against Christianity, but did not really understand the problems of his own beliefs. So I said, "Am I not correct in saying that on the basis of your system, cruelty and non-cruelty are ultimately equal, that there is no intrinsic difference between them?" He agreed. ... the student, in whose room we met, who had clearly understood the implications of what the Sikh had admitted, picked up his kettle of boiling water with which he was about to make tea, and stood with it steaming over the Indian's head. The man looked up and asked him what he was doing and he said, with a cold yet gentle finality, "There is no difference between cruelty and non-cruelty." Thereupon the Hindu walked out into the night.[23]

Samuel M. Thompson's brilliant philosophical critique on pantheism deserves our attention. The philosopher writes:

- Any attempt to identify God and the world is bound to fail just so far as it recognizes the slightest distinction between the world as such and God as such; for any distinction whatever is enough to destroy the identity. On the other hand if there is no distinction then we do not have two things to identify with each other, and so again the basic pantheistic doctrine fails.[24]

There is much wisdom in the words of J. I. Packer, "If God's being is an aspect of my own, 'the depth in me,' all attempts to worship Him become self-worship."[25] At this point one can hardly avoid the temptation of citing Professor C. E. M. Joad's eloquent remarks:

- If there is only God, how can there be illusions? Can God's mind create and nourish them? No. Can mine? I think that it can. But, if it can, my mind must be other than God's, and all is not God.[26]

Dr. E. Stanley Jones' insightful truism must not escape our notice:

- I have searched India from the Himalaya to Cape Cormorin for over a half century to find a person who has arrived at the realization of the self and become the Self, become God. I have never found one. It is illusion. ... A creature can never become the Creator.[27]

2. REALITY IS ILLOGICAL

Basic to all eastern thinking is that reality is illogical and reason cannot lead to God. It is often asserted that "God is greater than logic." Buddha's advice to his disciples was, "Do not go by reasoning, nor by inferring, nor by argument."[28] It is said, "The Buddha preached for forty-nine years and in all that time found it not necessary to speak one word."[29] Writing on Zen Buddhism, D. T. Suzuki points out, "Zen is one thing and logic another. When we fail to make this distinction and expect Zen to give us something logically consistent and intellectually illuminating, we altogether misinterpret the signification of Zen."[30] Suzuki goes far in asserting,

"All our theorization fails to touch reality."[31] Sopwith Camel rightly expressed the eastern approach in a song that said, "Stamp out reality before reality stamps out you."[32] Abby Hoffman argued along the same line when he wrote in his book, *Revolution for the Hell of It*, "Listen to touches, Listen to silence . . . Don't listen to words, Don't listen to words. Don't listen to words." For the East the mind is a drunken monkey. Hare Krishna members speak about the garbage-pail mind.[33]

Reason has no essence in eastern thinking. It insists, "Don't think, when you are thinking that you are thinking." We are told, "Shiva gave birth to Shakti and Shakti gave birth to Shiva. But only the sages can comprehend this secret." Guru Maharaji Ji contends, "Mind always projects what is false. Mind is a black light."[34]

The Hindu argues that God is both personal and impersonal, Shankara, the impersonal, and Ramanuja, the personal. W. Cantwell Smith reminds us, "No Hindu has said anything that some other Hindu has not contradicted."[35] The Hindu is not embarrassed that his concept violates the law of the excluded middle in logic. He considers God totally other, far removed, contrary to all our thinking. God is everything our mind cannot conceive. The *Upanishads* suggest:

■ Him (Brahman) the eye does not see, nor the tongue express, nor the mind grasp. Him we neither know nor are able to teach. Different is he from the known, and . . . from the unknown. . . .

  He truly knows Brahman who knows him as beyond knowledge; he who thinks that he knows, knows not. The ignorant think that Brahman is known, but the wise know him to be beyond knowledge.[36]

This irrational approach to reality is so typical of the Zen movement. An ancient Zen master would lift one of his fingers whenever he was asked the meaning of Zen – this was his answer. Others would slap the inquirer or kick a ball. A Zen student says, "I owe everything to my teacher because he taught me nothing." According to them, "When you don't understand, then you will know." This is in keeping with Lao-tse's famous aphorism, "He who knows doesn't speak; he who speaks doesn't know." One Zen master goes so far as saying, "When the mouth opens, all are wrong."[37] Shankara, the famous Hindu philosopher, illustrates the eastern agnosticism:

■ **"Sir," said a pupil to his master, "teach me the nature of Brahman." The master did not reply. When a second and a third time he was importuned, he answered, "I teach you indeed, but you do not follow. His name is silence."**[38]

The problem with the notion that "reality is illogical" is not immediately apparent when one accepts the notion without reflection. Conditioned to think in this way, people seldom question the validity of the premise. If reality is illogical, how could one know reality? If reality is totally irrational, how does one differentiate between reality and fantasy? The eastern mystic Lao-tse points this out, "If, when I was asleep I was a man dreaming I was a butterfly, how do I know when I am awake I am not a butterfly dreaming I am a man?" How could one judge falsity from truth if one cannot comprehend rationally? If God were beyond my conception, then the very concept that 'God is one' would be meaningless.

7

"If, when I was
asleep I was a
man dreaming I
was a butterfly,
how do I know
when I am
awake I am not
a butterfly
dreaming I am a
man?"

Lao-tse, Zen master

What does one possibly understand by the following statement that was attributed to Buddha?

■ **I have not elucidated that the world is eternal, and I have not elucidated that the world is not eternal. I have not elucidated that the saint exists after death, I have not elucidated that the saint does not exist after death. I have not elucidated that the saint both exists and does not exist after death.**[39]

These esoteric statements sound very profound and impressive, but no one understands what they mean, not even the guru who makes them. R. C. Sproul puts this delightfully:

■ **Absurdities often sound profound because they are incapable of being understood. When we hear things we do not understand, sometimes we think they are simply too deep or weighty for us to grasp when in fact they are merely unintelligible statements like "one-hand clapping."**[40]

Pantheists can't live consistently with their premise. If reality is illogical, why speak and write on reality? To speak and write one must use logic, without which no communication is possible. If the pantheist is not saying anything logical about ultimate reality, why should anyone follow the pantheist? Why is he advocating pantheism, and not theism or atheism? If logic does not matter, why not accept any other belief system? It is at this point that pantheism reveals its serious inconsistency. The position of the pantheist is either self-refuting or meaningless – there is no third possibility. If there is such a third possibility, is that rational? If it is not, then it's irrational. It makes no sense to speak of a third category which transcends reason when the pantheist offers no evidence of ever crossing it. The Oxford scholar C. S. Lewis declares, "Unless human reasoning is valid, no science can be true."[41]

If reality is not rational, then this statement, which says reality is not rational, is either saying something rational about reality or is not saying anything rational about reality. If it is not saying anything rational about reality, then the pantheist in reality has said nothing about reality. If the statement is saying something true about reality, then reality is not beyond reason. For if it is beyond reason, how could the pantheist make reasonable statements of that which is beyond reason? If reality is unreasonable, then one has no basis for making reasonable statements about reality. A professor

once started his class by saying, "Today our topic is 'The Inadequacy of Language,'" and he proceeded with his lecture. After some time a student raised his hand and said, "Professor, if language is inadequate, it would be pointless for us to sit here and listen to your words." Another student understood the problem and stood up and proposed, "Yes! We are wasting our time if language is an inadequate tool for communication. We better leave this place and play squash." One by one the students left the class, leaving the professor lecturing to himself. If words and reasons are inadequate, why use them at all? R. C. Sproul is right, "When the laws of logic are violated, intelligible communication ceases."[42]

If God is beyond all thought, he is beyond the thought that he is beyond all thought. And he is beyond this thought as well and also the thought that this is so. If it is true that God is beyond thought, then the thought which says, "God is beyond thought" is not true, hence it is false to say God is beyond thought. We cannot give a rational account of that which is absolutely irrational, for then the irrational would be rational, and it would not be absolutely irrational. If reality is totally irrational, then how did I get to know so much about reality in order to make rational statements about ultimate reality? When logic is murdered, one is forced to attend the funeral of truth. The death of truth is inevitable when logic and common sense are abandoned.

Very often, in order to justify their position, pantheistic mystics assert that their views could be expressed only in symbols. But under close analysis, this approach is no better. Professor C. E. M. Joad, after examining this position, concludes:

■ **I have never been able to make anything of symbolism. A symbol I understand to be a sign for something else. Either the symbolist knows what the something else is, in which case I cannot see why he should not tell us what it is straight out, instead of obscurely hinting at it in symbols, or he does not, in which case not knowing what the symbols stand for he cannot expect his readers to find out for him. Usually, I suspect, he does not, and his symbolism is merely a device to conceal his muddled thinking.[43]**

If a belief system is logically incoherent, then it fails to pass the test for truth. It provides no sensible ground for belief. Philosopher H. J. Paton's wisdom is much needed at this point, "To declare war upon reason is to alienate all who care for truth and to hold open the door for the imposter and the zealot."[44]

3. REALITY IS EXPERIENCE

Since pantheists say reality is irrational and the mind is incapable of conceiving reality, the door to reality is experience. The major emphasis of eastern religion is meditation: looking into one's own nature, learning to control consciousness, becoming part of the cosmic oneness, losing one's identity, and being one with the one. Mahatma Gandhi once told his followers to "turn the spotlight inward." A guru once told the British Christian sociologist Os Guinness:

■ **To the Christian, talk of God is rather like the great bulk of an iceberg, whereas his experience of God is only the tiny tip of the iceberg; but for the Easterner the experience of**

God is the bulk of the iceberg, whereas his talk about God is only the tip.[45]

Alan Watts, the leading advocate of Zen Buddhism, asserts, "It is one's own spiritual realization that makes the difference and the mind is its own place, and of itself can make a heaven of hell, a hell of heaven."[46] Sohaku Ogata in his *Zen for the West* writes:

■ **The eye by which I see God is the same eye by which God sees me. My eye and God's are one and the same – one in seeing, one in knowing and one in loving . . . . When I have shut the doors of my five senses, earnestly desiring God, I find him in my soul as clearly and as joyful as he is in eternity. . . . Meditation, high thinking, and union with God, have drawn me to heaven.[47]**

The *Upanishads* express that the non-rational final experience "Turiya" (the state of highest blessedness):

■ **Is not that which is conscious of the inner world . . . nor the outer world . . . nor both. It is not simple consciousness nor is it unconsciousness. It is unperceived, unrelated, incomprehensible, uninferable, unthinkable, and undescribable . . . it is the cessation of all phenomena; it is all peace, all bliss, non-dual.[48]**

The underlying presupposition behind the view that reality can only be experienced is the notion that experience proves reality. But does subjective experience prove what we believe? When we reflect on experience it is worth remembering the remark of philosopher Bertrand Russell, "We can make no distinction between the man who eats little and sees heaven and the man who drinks much and sees snakes." People who seek to prove their metaphysical beliefs on the basis of experience think metaphysics and experience are synonymous. What they fail to see is that experience is something one has and metaphysics is the interpretation of that experience. One should also remember that experiences are capable of many interpretations.

No experience is, in the final analysis, self-interpreting. People with eastern religious experience often say, "I had an experience but I cannot describe it to you." Persons with this mentality fail to see that experiences are meaningless unless describable. In other words, how can you know what you don't know? Experience is too weak a base on which to build one's eternal destiny. Followers of religions from Zen Buddhism to Mormonism have all used subjective experience to back up their beliefs. The fact that their beliefs conflict with one another disproves the claim that experience could validate one's belief system. An experience could be any number of things. It could be psychological, physiological, biblical, or even demonic. Theologian Clark Pinnock substantiates this mode of thinking when he writes:

■ **Religious sensation by itself can only prove itself. The assertion "God exists" simply does not follow from the assertion "I had an experience of God." A psychological datum cannot automatically lead to a metaphysical discovery. However unique an experience may be, it is capable of a number of radically differing interpretations. It may be only an encounter with one's own subconscious.**[49]

Our psychological experience must be supported by objective, external criteria in order to validate our belief system. Professor Joad's insight is particularly valuable when he contrasts knowledge (truth) and feeling (experience). He wisely points out:

■ **Now the reason why knowledge is communicable and feeling is not is to be found in the fact that knowledge is of something other than and external to itself, whereas feeling reports nothing but the fact of the feeling. Knowledge, in short, involves a reference to something else, namely, that which is known; feeling does not.**[50]

At this point Paul T. Arveson's eloquent response to eastern metaphysics should be noted, "Only when the axis of truth-value is accepted is it possible to communicate, live, and share in a society."[51] By starting from experience one simply has no means of checking his or her experience, for the simple reason that a subjective experience is too soft a ground to build the foundation of one's eternal hope. Subjectivism cannot be the basis for truth. "What we learn from experience," argues C. S. Lewis, "depends on the kind of philosophy we bring to experience. It is therefore useless to appeal to experience before we have settled, as well as we can, the philosophical question."[52] Dr. Walter Pahnke rightly suggests, "It is misleading even to use the words 'I experienced' since during the peak of experience . . . there was no duality between myself and what I experienced."[53] Carl Jung's striking remarks should be heeded, "We can never decide definitely whether a person is really enlightened, or whether he merely imagines it, we have no criterion of this."[54] How can one be sure that it is God he is experiencing and not the devil, the Holy Spirit and not an evil spirit?

Besides the above reason, one should also carefully consider the element of psychological and spiritual dangers. When one totally depends on the sensuous, one may end up being senseless. Mystical experience is extremely dangerous, as William J. Petersen indicates, "The founder of the Krishna sect, Chaitanya, 'danced in such ecstasy, repeating the name of Hare, that he danced on into the sea at Puri and was drowned.'"[55] Masters and Houston wisely remark:

■ **The history of transcendental experience bears testimony to the thin line that often separates the sublime from the demonic, and to the frequency with which the one may cross over into the other.**[56]

The danger of mystical experience should not be overlooked. Consider the experience of Julio Ruibal, a former yoga master and guru who finally came to understand the powers of darkness in mystical experience. His comment is worth noting:

■ **I advanced in the occult sphere so fast that I soon became the youngest guru in the Western Hemisphere, and one of the most advanced and powerful. Twice a week I taught yoga on television. Hatha-Yoga sounds like a nice simple set of exercises; everyone thinks it is just gymnastics. I want to warn that it is just the beginning of a devilish trap. After I became an instructor in Hatha-Yoga, my guru showed me that the only thing these exercises do is open your appetite for the occult. They are like marijuana; they usually lead you on to a drug that is worse and stronger, binding you so completely that only Christ can deliver you. Many people think that occult power is just the power of the mind. This is not true. There is a point beyond which the power of the mind ends and the demonic power takes over.**[57]

159

The wisdom of Princeton theologian B. B. Warfield is remarkably relevant to those who are seeking for God in the wrong direction: "**He who begins by seeking God within himself may end by confusing himself with God.**"[58] Divinity is not in humanity. Looking for God in man is like looking at yourself in the mirror and saying, "Here is God." Man beginning with himself has no basis of knowing the validity of his experience. Unless God has revealed himself objectively and given us the content of his revelation, humans are lost and live in darkness.

III. THE CHRISTIAN ANSWER

The credibility of a religion depends on the justifiability of its truth claims. There are three basic criteria we commonly employ to determine the validity and truthfulness of a world view. These criteria affirm that in order for a religion to be true it must be:

1. Logically Consistent,
2. Factually Verifiable,
3. Existentially Liveable.

It is meaningless to say that reality is beyond logic or that religion is a matter of faith and devoid of reason, for this very statement presupposes logic. Every meaningful statement is either logical or illogical. If it is logical then reality is logical, but if the statement is not logical then it is meaningless, for a meaningless statement affirms nothing. David Freeman notes, "**If beliefs are to make sense they must be consistent and not contradictory.**"[59]

The Christian faith is logically consistent, for it affirms the logically possible. Absurdities which are expressed in Hinduism and Buddhism (e.g. only God exists, the world is an illusion, no individuality, evil is an illusion, etc.) are not found in Christianity. The logical basis of Christianity is carefully argued in the writings of Thomas Aquinas, Augustine, James Buswell, G. H. Clark, E. J. Carnell, C. Stephen Evans, David Freeman, Stuart Hackett, William Hasker, C. F. H. Henry, Peter Kreeft, C. S. Lewis, Ronald Nash, Alvin Plantinga, Richard Purtill, David L. Wolfe, William Young, and others.

Secondly, the Christian faith is grounded and rooted in history. Unlike eastern religion which bases its teachings on abstract concepts, Christianity presents the reality of a living Christ who died and rose again for the salvation and liberation of man from sin. The facts of Christ and his resurrection are historically verifiable like all other historical events that are verifiable. The works of J. W. Montgomery, F. F. Bruce, C. H. Pinnock, C. Blomberg, William Craig, G. Habermas, J. P. Moreland, Bernard Ramm, William Ramsay, and others indicate beyond reasonable doubt that the Christian faith is based on good historical evidence.

Finally, the Christian world view is existentially liveable. Christianity affirms the reality of a universe which has meaning, purpose, and order. Everyone lives on the basis of the Christian concept of reality, although few believe it. The point is that we must be able to live what we believe and believe what we live. Fine minds like G. K. Chesterton, F. Schaeffer, Os Guinness, H. Blamires, C. Van Til, and others have provided excellent insights on how Christianity fits the facts of human life and experience.

Christianity provides a resource for the dignity, the morality, and the worthwhileness of humanity. Human beings are not just a cosmic accident, a speck of dust, or a drop of water in an impersonal ocean. We are created in the image of God and are designed to have a meaningful relationship with our Creator. Professor Paul Krishna, a former Hindu, testifies to the reality of the resource found in Christ:

■ **As a Hindu I endured self-discipline and much study for one purpose – to better myself, to achieve heaven by my own deeds. Christianity starts with man's weakness. It asks us to accept our selfishness and inabilities, then promises a new nature. Christ came to heal the sick, not the well or self-sufficient.**[60]

Human beings need not despair and go on an eternal search for the Eternal, for the Eternal has come to the temporal: Jesus said, "I have come that they may have life, and have it to the full" (John 10:10 NIV).

Muslims do not read the Quran
and conclude that it is divine;
rather they believe that it is divine,
and then they read it.

WILFRED CANTWELL SMITH

The Word did not become Flesh:
the Word became a Book.

HENDRIK KRAEMER

Islam confronts
what is immutable in God
with what is permanent
in man.

FRITHJOF SCHUON

ANSWERING THE CHALLENGE OF ISLAM

8

IN a significant article on Islam, *Time* magazine declares, "Muslims are rediscovering their spiritual roots and reasserting the political power of the Islamic way of life." *Time* goes on to say, "The West can no longer afford to ignore or dismiss the living power of the prophet's message."[1]

Islam is making a great impact, both religiously and politically, around the globe. The continuing crisis in the Middle East illustrates the reality of its existence. "God may be dead in the West," asserts one observer, "but He is very much alive in the Middle East."

From Malaysia to Morocco converts are being won to the Islamic faith. New centers for the propagation of Islam are emerging around the world. In some parts of Africa, Muslims are winning ten times as many converts as Christians. Islam is increasingly becoming one of the world's most popular religions and the fastest-growing faith in the 20th century. In numbers of followers, it is second only to Christianity. It is estimated that one out of every five persons on earth now profess to be a Muslim – about 967 million. It is increasingly becoming the religion of the Near and Far East with growing numbers of adherents in both Europe and America. In the light of this, one should not ignore the reality of its existence nor dismiss its power of influence in our present century.

The American theologian Bruce Demarest writes:

■ **Through such movements as the World Community of Islam, the religion of Mohammed is vigorously contending** today for the souls of America. It boldly claims to possess the answers to evils such as alcoholism, promiscuity, the breakdown of the family, and racism that plague American life.[2]

The Islamic scholar Don M. McCurry observes, "In country after country orthodox Muslims are awakening, flexing their muscles, and becoming more militant."[3] During a recent well-financed "Festival of Islam" in Britain, Muslims strongly affirmed, "Unless we win London over to Islam, we will fail to win the whole of the Western world."

Islam, like Judaism and Christianity, claims to be the climax of divine revelation. The source of this revelation is the Qur'an. In his popular work, *Understanding Islam*, Frithjof Schuon epitomizes the Islamic approach:

■ **If the Qur'an contains elements of polemic concerning Christianity and, for stronger reasons, concerning Judaism, it is because Islam came after these religions, and this means that it was obliged . . . to put itself forward as an improvement on what came before it.[4]**

The Muslim believes that the Qur'an is the Word of God given to their prophet Mohammed who is regarded as the greatest and the last (or seal) of the prophets. The Qur'an presents Adam, Noah, Abraham, Moses, Jesus, and the other biblical characters as genuine prophets of God. Jesus Christ is given great titles, but his divinity is rejected. In many cases Jesus is presented in unusual terms and set forth as being superior to all other prophets; however, Mohammed is accepted as the final prophet.

The teachings of Islam are summarized in the Five Doctrines and the Five Pillars. J. N. D. Anderson points out, "It is these Five Pillars, and particularly the profession of the creed and the performance of prayer and fasting, which chiefly make up the practice of Islam to the average Muslim."[5]

I. THE RELIABILITY OF THE NEW TESTAMENT

Muslims believe that the Bible was corrupted by the early Christians. They argue that false ideas and teaching were introduced into the Scriptures, thus distorting the original teachings of Jesus Christ. They teach that "The ungodly ones among them changed that word into another than that which had been told them" (7:162). It says, "Woe to those who write the Book with their own hands, And then say: 'This is from God,' to traffic with it for a miserable price!" (2:79).

Maurice Bucaille, an Islamic apologist, writes, "As for the Gospels nobody can claim that they invariably contain faithful accounts of Jesus' words or a description of His actions strictly in keeping with reality."[6] In his book, *Muhammad and Christ*, Maulvi Muhammad Ali asserts, "The basis of Christian religion is based on the most unreliable record."[7] Bucaille goes so far as to say, "We do not in fact have an eye witness account from the life of Jesus, contrary to what many Christians imagine."[8]

Contrary to popular opinion, the New Testament is supported by a wealth of manuscripts – unlike most classical documents. F. F. Bruce, the New Testament scholar, writes:

> ■ **The evidence for our New Testament writing is ever so much greater than the evidence for many writings of classical authors, the authenticity of which no-one dreams of questioning.**[9]

The New Testament is unusual in its accuracy, history, and archaeology. Leading textual scholars who have studied the materials conclude that they are reliable. This conviction is shared, not only by those who maintain a conservative position, but even by those who come from the radical left. One such scholar is John A. T. Robinson, whose radical theology is well expressed in his popular volume, *Honest to God*. In 1976 Robinson authored a book, *Re-Dating the New Testament*, which shocked the scholarly world. His research provided many evidences for the reliability of the New Testament.

Professor Joachim Jeremias makes a valuable comment concerning the authenticity of the New Testament:

> ■ **The linguistic and stylistic evidence shows so much faithfulness and such respect towards the tradition of the sayings of Jesus that we are justified in drawing up the following principle of method: in the synoptic tradition it is the inauthenticity, and not the authenticity, of the sayings of Jesus that must be demonstrated.**[10]

These facts provide good reason for one to accept the authenticity of the New Testament. Clark Pinnock is right, "Pessimism concerning the trustworthiness of the New Testament is utterly unwarranted, and generally reflects ignorance of the facts."[11]

The Christian is in a far better position to argue for the New Testament than the Muslim is for his Qur'an. In his work, *The Sacred Writings of the World's Great Religions*, Dr. S. E. Frost writes:

> ■ **Consequently, some twelve years later Othman, third Caliph, commanded that all copies of the original work be destroyed and a new authentic version be prepared. This accepted volume contains scraps of beliefs from many religious sources, chief of which are Arabic traditions and folklore, Zoroastrianism, the Jewish and Christian theology.**[12]

Josh McDowell and John Gilchrist assert:

■ **There is concrete evidence in the best works of Islamic tradition (e.g. the Sahih of Muslim, the Sahih of Bukhari, the Mishkat-ul-Masabih), that from the start the Qur'an had numerous variant and conflicting readings.**[13]

II. THE RATIONALITY OF THE TRINITY

Although there may be many similarities between Islam and Christianity, there is nothing which divides the two religions more radically than their views of God. A well-educated Muslim once told a Christian, "Whenever you Christians speak of Jesus as the 'Son of God' it makes our blood boil."[14] The Muslim view of God is expressed in seven words: *La ilaha illa Allah, Mohammed rasul Allah* – "There is no god but Allah (and) Mohammed is the prophet of Allah." This is their fundamental conviction of God. Just to repeat this creed *ipso facto* makes one a true believer.

According to philosopher David Freeman, "The fundamental conception of Allah or God is impersonal and negative. He is a vast monad that has no resemblance to anything known or to any creature." He further adds, "God is so different from his creatures that very little can be postulated of him."[15] The Qur'an in Sura 112 points out, "There is not to him a single equal." This idea is well expressed in a popular song, "Whatsoever your mind can conceive, That Allah is not, you may believe." God is totally other, and there is nothing by which he can be compared. If this be the case, then in the Islamic context God is totally unknowable. William McElwee Miller is right:

> ■ Such a God is therefore unknowable, for all that can be said of Him is that He is not this or that. While God's name is often on the lips of Moslems, He is to most of them an unknown Being.[16]

Miller agrees with Raymond Lull, the first great missionary to Muslims, "The greatest deficiency in the Moslem religion is in its conception of God."[17]

Christians share with the Muslims in their denial of polytheism – the pantheon of numerous gods. Mohammed is right, that if Christians believe in three gods they are no better. But this is where the founder of Islam sadly misunderstood Christianity. Thomas Hughes provides the reasons for this misunderstanding:

> ■ The controversies regarding the nature and person of our Divine Lord had begotten a sect of Tri-theists led by a Syrian philosopher named John Philoponus of Alexandria, and are sufficient to account for Muhammed's conception of the Blessed Trinity. The worship of the Virgin Mary had also given rise to a religious controversy between the Antiduo-Marianites and the Collyruduabs .... Under the circumstances, it is not surprising to find that the mind of the Arabian reformer turned away from Christianity and endeavoured to construct a religion on the lines of Judaism.[18]

Mohammed's misconception of the doctrine of the Trinity is equally transparent in the Qur'an. His notions about the Trinity are far removed from biblical evidence. The Qur'an clearly contradicts the central teaching of Holy Scriptures on the divinity of Christ. Sura 5:78 states, "Jesus Christ the son of Mary was no more than An Apostle." According to Phil Parshall:

> ■ Muslims generally believe the dynamic of the Trinity consists of God the Father's having sexual intercourse with Mary the mother of Jesus, who was the second member of the Trinity. This union resulted in the birth of Jesus as the third person of the Godhead.[19]

In Sura 4:171 Mohammed eloquently states Muslims' dominant attitude toward the Christian God:

8

"In country after country orthodox Muslims are awakening, flexing their muscles, and becoming more militant."

Don M. McCurry,
Islamic scholar

■ **O people of the Scripture! Do not exaggerate in your religion nor utter aught concerning Allah save the truth. The Messiah, Jesus son of Mary, was only a messenger of Allah, and His Word which He cast into Mary, and a spirit from Him. So believe in Allah and His messengers, and say not three – cease! (it is) better for you! Allah is only one God. Far is it removed from His transcendent majesty that He should have a son.**

The Muslims conceive God in terms of mathematical unity, hence reasoning from this point of view, God is by definition indivisible. The logic by which the Muslim reasons is as follows: If Father is God, The Son is God, and The Holy Spirit is God, mathematically the answer is three Gods (1 + 1 + 1 = 3).

But God is not a mathematical unity. By what right must God fit into our limited and finite category of mathematics? Is he not beyond the human perspective of existence? Should God exist in the same dimension as his creatures? Is he not greater than his creation? Do not the Muslims argue that Allah is unlike his creatures and there is nothing to equal him? If this is the case, why do the Muslims limit God to human dimension and limit God to the confines of their own understanding? God is not a man that he should fit into our categories. Robert Brow makes an important point, "**The Christian vision of the unity of God is not mathematical but rather organic. The electron, proton and neutron in the simplest atom are not added to make three, but held together by atomic force to form one unit.**" Hence, argues Brow, "**If God is a living God, we should not therefore be surprised to find a complexity within his unity.**"[20] Writing on the same subject Phil Parshall states:

■ **Aristotle pointed out that the word one is used in more than one sense. It can be used to indicate oneness of quantity or oneness of essence. For instance, a molecule of water may be "one" numerically without being one or single in its essence, as its formula H_2O indicates.[21]**

God is one in essence, but three in person. To put it in another way, in God there is one What and three Who. What is God? God is one in essence. Who is God? He is the Father, the Son, and the Holy Spirit.

The Trinity does not involve any contradiction, as some believe. It does not violate the laws of logic. It may go beyond logic but never against it. The Trinity is neither a metaphysical absurdity nor a mathematical nonsense. Very often the doctrine of the Trinity is rejected not because it is illogical but, as Dale Rhoton correctly observes, "One of the main reasons people object to the doctrine of the Trinity is that they automatically think of God as a Being with one centre of consciousness."[22] If we approach God with this disposition, our minds will always remain in the dark as to his truth and reality. We concur with the judgment of J. S. Wright:

■ **If we start with the fixed idea that the unity of the Godhead means a bare mathematical unity, and that the divine Son-ship inevitably means that the Father existed before the Son, Scripture then cannot be clear to us, since we have tried to fix it into an arbitrary pattern of thinking.[23]**

Dr. John W. Montgomery's insightful remarks on the subject are worthy of note:

■ **The doctrine of the Trinity is not "irrational"; what is irrational is to suppress the biblical evidence for Trinity in favor of Unity, or the evidence for Unity in favor of Trinity. Our data must take precedence over our models – or, stating it better, our models must sensitively reflect the full range of data.[24]**

The data of Scripture clearly points to a triune God. The greatest reason Christians accept the doctrine of the Trinity is that we cannot make sense of many important biblical passages unless the Trinity is true. The New Testament is meaningless without the concept of the Trinity. The fact is that God has revealed himself in the Bible as Father, Son, and Holy Spirit. The evidence for this is clearly revealed in the following verses: Matthew 28:19;

2 Corinthians 1:21–22; 13:14; 1 Corinthians 6:11; 12:4–6; Galatians 3:11–14; 1 Thessalonians 5:18–19; 1 Peter 1:2; cf. John 1:1–3; 10:30, 33; 14:9; 20:17; Colossians 2:9.

What puzzles the rational mind is not the doctrine of the Trinity, but the teaching of the Qur'an. Jesus Christ is presented as far superior to Mohammed in birth, title, deeds, power, and position, yet we are asked to follow Mohammed. The Jesus of the Qur'an is something of a mystery. Why is Jesus unique if Mohammed is the greatest prophet? Why is Jesus called the Messiah? Why was his birth miraculous if he was not the greatest of God's messengers?

III. THE REALITY OF THE RESURRECTION

The Christian faith is not based on an abstract metaphysical concept nor an illusory esoteric principle. Christianity is grounded and rooted in an important historical space-time event – the death and the resurrection of Jesus Christ. It is not views but news: the good news, that God in Jesus Christ has visited our planet and has solved our problem of sin and death.

The apostle Paul in a significant chapter in the book of First Corinthians states, "If Christ has not been raised, your faith is futile; you are still in your sins. . . . If only for this life we have hope in Christ, we are to be pitied more than all men" (15:17, 19 NIV). Unlike Islam, Christianity appeals to historical facts and evidence to authenticate its claims and credibility. But Islam denies these claims and rejects the evidence. The Qur'an says, "But they killed him not, nor crucified him, but so it was made to appear to them" (4:157). Agreeing with this verse Yusuf Ali points out, "The Quranic teaching is that Christ was not crucified, nor killed by the Jews, notwithstanding certain apparent circumstances which produced that illusion in the minds of some of his enemies."[25] It is the basic conviction of most Muslims that Jesus never died on the cross. They are uncertain as to what actually took place, but they emphatically deny his death on the cross.

Maulvi Muhammad Ali rightly sees the logic of the Christian position but wrongly denies its evidences. He writes:

■ **Christ never died on the cross and he never rose from the dead: the preaching of the Christian missionary is therefore vain and vain is also his faith. The Christian religion laid its foundation on the death of Christ on the cross and his subsequent rising; both these statements have been proved to be utterly wrong.[26]**

It stands to reason that if Christ did not die and rise from the dead, then the Christian faith is utterly false, but if Christ did rise from the dead, then logic dictates that Christianity is the truth.

The Muslim's rejection of the crucifixion is illogical and has no basis in history. This position actually poses more problems and creates numerous absurdities. One can maintain this position only at the expense of facts and evidences. This view implies that the Roman soldiers who were responsible for the death of Jesus were careless and irresponsible. Dr. John W. Montgomery rightly points out:

■ **Jesus surely died on the cross, for Roman crucifixion teams knew their business (they had enough practice). He could not possibly have rolled the heavy boulder from the door of the tomb after the crucifixion experience.**[27]

The evidence for the resurrection of Christ is unbeatable. Those who examined the evidence with an open mind have been persuaded to believe it. Lord Caldecote, Lord Chief Justice of England, wrote after examining the evidence, "The claims of Jesus Christ, namely His resurrection, has led me as often as I have tried to examine the evidence to believe it as a fact beyond dispute."[28] Lord Lyndhurst was one of the greatest legal minds in the history of England. He was three times High Chancellor of England and was elected High Steward of Cambridge University. His verdict on the resurrection is, "I know pretty well what evidence is; and, I tell you, such evidence as that for the Resurrection has never broken down yet."[29]

The British lawyer, Frank Morison, set out to write a book that would finally refute the resurrection. Thinking that the resurrection was nothing but a fairy tale, he started his research, but after months of carefully sifting through the evidence he was forced to the opposite conclusion. He fell on his knees and accepted Christ as his own personal, living Savior. He then wrote a book with the title, *Who Moved the Stone?*, with the first chapter entitled, "The Book that Refused to be Written." He could not logically refute the evidence but was forced by the facts to embrace the truth of the resurrection.[30]

The existence of Islam indicates man's search for answers, but no matter

how hard he tries he will never in Islam find the answer. Unless God personally reveals his truth, man will forever remain in the dark regarding the purpose of his life and the meaning of his ultimate existence. The answer to Islam is the same answer which Christians have found in Jesus Christ. A former Muslim, Daud Rahbar, professor in the Islamic Department of Punjab University in Pakistan, answers the question of every Muslim:

> ■ **If the Biblical narrative about Jesus is a myth and if the Creator is other than that Divine Martyr Jesus, then He is a Creator who ought to vacate His heavenly throne for the Superior Being Jesus. But the truth is that the Eternal Creator and the Divine Martyr Jesus are one and the same Being.[31]**

CHAPTER NOTES

CHAPTER I

1. The Federal Bureau of Investigation statistics indicate that since 1960 there has been a 560% increase in violent crime in the U.S.A. The National Center for Health Statistics indicates divorce rates have tripled and the number of children living with single parents has also tripled. The teenage suicide rate has increased by 200%.
2. Victor Frankl, *The Unheard Cry for Meaning* (New York: Simon & Schuster, 1978), 20–21.
3. Erich Fromm, *Zen Buddhism and Psychoanalysis* (New York: Harper & Row, 1960), 85–86.
4. For an excellent discussion of the concept of God, see Carl F. H. Henry, *God, Revelation and Authority* (Waco, Tex.: Word, 1976), E. L. Mascall, *Existence and Analogy* (London: Longmans, Green, 1949), Thomas V. Morris, *Our Idea of God* (Downers Grove: InterVarsity, 1991), Ronald Nash, *The Concept of God* (Grand Rapids: Zondervan, 1983), H. P. Owen, *Christian Theism: A Study in Its Basic Principles* (Edinburgh: T. & T. Clark, 1984), Alvin Plantinga, *God and Other Minds: A Study of the Rational Justification of Belief in God* (Ithaca, N.Y.: Cornell University Press, 1967), Keith Ward, *Rational Theology and the Creativity of God* (New York: Pilgrim, 1982), Keith E. Yandell, *Christianity and Philosophy* (Grand Rapids: Eerdmans, 1984).
5. The writings of famous atheists like Nietzsche, Bertrand Russell, Sartre, Albert Camus, and Hemingway confirm this truth.
6. Quoted in Batsell Barrett Baxter, *I Believe Because …* (Grand Rapids: Baker, 1978), 29.
7. Mortimer Adler, *Great Books of the Western World* (ed. Robert M. Hutchins; Chicago: Encyclopaedia Britannica, 1955), 2.561.
8. See Hans Küng, *Does God Exist?* (trans. by Edward Quinn; Garden City, N.Y.: Doubleday, 1980).
9. See John M. Frame, *The Doctrine of the Knowledge of God* (Phillipsburg, N.J.: Presbyterian & Reformed, 1987).
10. The category fallacy made prominent by philosopher G. Ryle is committed when things or facts of one category are regarded as having similar properties to another (e.g. color to sound, truth to questions, space to time). It would be a category mistake to ask: What does yellow taste like? Can you show me the sound of music? Who made God?
11. Many important philosophers and scientists conclude that the scientific method is not capable of handling all realities. See Gordon H. Clark, *The Philosophy of Science and Belief in God* (Nutley, N.J.: Craig, 1964), R. Hooykaas, *Religion and the Rise of Modern Science* (Edinburgh: Scottish Academic, 1972), Stanley Jaki, *The Road of Science and the Ways to God* (Chicago: University of Chicago Press, 1978), T. S. Kuhn, *The Structure of Scientific Revolutions* (Chicago: University of Chicago Press, 1970), E. L. Mascall, *Christian Theology and Natural Science* (London: Longmans, Green, 1956).
12. Plato, *Apology*, 38
13. D. Elton Trueblood, *General Philosophy* (Grand Rapids: Baker, 1963), 209.
14. J. L. Mackie, *The Miracle of Theism* (Oxford: Clarendon, 1982), 1.
15. Edward Sillem, *Ways of Thinking About God* (London: Darton, Longman & Todd, 1961), 1.
16. C. Stephen Evans, *The Quest for Faith: Pointers to God* (Leicester: InterVarsity, 1986), 131.
17. *Time*, April 7, 1980, 65.
18. Not long ago Alvin Plantinga, arguably one of the brightest philosophers of our time, presented a paper "Two Dozen (or So) Theistic Arguments" at a philosophical conference and complained that our philosophers have not availed themselves of the rich material that supports a theistic universe. See also the essay by Henry

Schaeffer III, "Stephen Hawking, The Big Bang, and God."

19. For an in-depth discussion on this evidence see Donald R. Burrill, ed., *The Cosmological Arguments: A Spectrum of Opinion* (Garden City, N.Y.: Anchor, 1967), William Lane Craig, *The Kalam Cosmological Argument* (New York: Barnes & Noble, 1979), Reginald Garrigou-Lagrange, *God: His Existence and Essence* (St. Louis: Herder, 1934), Norman L. Geisler and Winfried Corduan, *Philosophy of Religion* (Grand Rapids: Baker, 1989), Stuart Hackett, *The Resurrection of Theism* (Chicago: Moody), Eric Mascall, *He Who Is* (London: Longmans & Todd, 1966), Bruce R. Reichenbach, *The Cosmological Argument* (Springfield, Ill.: Charles Thomas, 1972), William L. Rowe, *The Cosmological Argument* (Princeton: Princeton University Press, 1975), R. C. Sproul, John Gerstner, and Arthur Lindsley, *Classical Apologetics* (Grand Rapids: Zondervan, 1984), Samuel M. Thompson, *A Modern Philosophy of Religion* (Chicago: Henry Regnery, 1955).

20. John Hick, *Christianity at the Centre* (London: SCM, 1968), 63.

21. H. D. Lewis, "Philosophy of Religion, History of," in *The Encyclopedia of Philosophy* (ed. Paul Edwards; New York: Macmillan, 1972), 6.284.

22. G. W. Leibniz, "The Principles of Nature and of Grace, Based on Reason," *Leibniz Selections* (ed. Philip P. Weiner, The Modern Student's Library; New York: Charles Scribner's Sons, 1951), 527.

23. Paul Tillich, *Systematic Theology* (Chicago: University of Chicago Press, 1963).

24. Ludwig Wittgenstein, *Tractatus Logico-Philosophicus* (London: Routledge & Kegan Paul, 1969), 149.

25. David Hugh Freeman, *A Philosophical Study of Religion* (Nutley, N.J.: Craig, 1964), 78.

26. John Warwick Montgomery, *How Do We Know There Is a God?* (Minneapolis: Bethany Fellowship, 1973), 9.

27. E. Sillem, op. cit.,182.

28. Fredrick Copleston, *The Existence of God* (ed. John Hick; New York: Macmillan, 1968), 174.

29. Colin Brown, *Philosophy and the Christian Faith* (London: Tyndale, 1969), 29.

30. "David Hume to John Stewart," February 1754, *The Letters of David Hume* (ed. J. Y. T. Greig; Oxford: Clarendon, 1932), 1.187.

31. Robert Gange, *Origins and Destiny* (Waco, Tex.: Word, 1986), 8.

32. Ibid.

33. *Los Angeles Times*, June 25, 1978, Part VI, 1, 6.

34. Although Einstein believed in the God of Spinoza who reveals himself in the orderly harmony of what exists, he was not an atheist by any stretch of the imagination. Einstein wrote, "God Himself *could not have* arranged those connections (expressed in scientific laws) in any other way than that which factually exists." (Quoted in Steven Winberg, *Dreams of a Final Theory* [New York: Random House, Pantheon, 1992], 242.)

35. J. P. Moreland and Kai Nielsen, *Does God Exist?* (Nashville: Thomas Nelson, 1990), 35.

36. Stanley L. Jaki, *Cosmos and Creator* (Edinburgh: Scottish Academy Press, 1980), 42.

37. David Hume, *Dialogues Concerning Natural Religion* (Indianapolis: Bobbs-Merrill, 1946), 214.

38. Quoted in *Heroes of History* (W. Frankford, Ill.: Caleb, 1992), 4.34.

39. Quoted in William Lane Craig, *Reasonable Faith: Christian Truth and Apologetics* (Wheaton: Crossway, 1994), 84.

40. Ibid., 83.

41. Immanuel Kant, *Critique of Pure Reason* (trans. by N. K. Smith; New York: St. Martin's, 1965), A. 623, B. 651.

42. Moreland and Nielsen, op. cit.,35.

43. See Roy Abraham Varghese, ed., *The Intellectuals Speak Out About God* (Chicago: Henry Regnery, 1984).

44. Ernst Chain, *Social Responsiblity and the Scientist in Modern Western Society* (London: Council of Christians and Jews, 1970), 25–26.

45. Paul Davies, *God and the New Physics* (New York: Simon & Schuster, 1983), 189.

46. Quoted in "How It All Began" in *Christianity Today*, August 1988, p. 32.

47. Richard Taylor, *Metaphysics* (Englewood Cliffs, N.J.: Prentice Hall, 1983), 99–102.

48. Richard Dawkins, "The Necessity of Darwinism," *New Scientist*, Vol. 94, April 15, 1982, 130.

49. Norman Geisler, *False Gods of Our Time* (Eugene, Ore.: Harvest House, 1985), 52.

50. Clark H. Pinnock, *Reason Enough: A Case for the Christian Faith* (Downers Grove: InterVarsity, 1980), 60.

51. Charles H. Malik, *The Wonder of Being* (Waco, Tex.: Word, 1974), 33.

52. Quoted in Norman L. Geisler, *Philosophy of Religion* (Grand Rapids: Zondervan, 1974), 116.

53. For further discussion on the moral argument, see Robert M. Adams, *The Virtue of Faith* (New York: Oxford University Press, 1987), "Moral Arguments for Theistic Belief," *Rationality and Religious Belief* (ed. by C. F. Delaney; South Bend, Ind.: University of Notre Dame Press, 1979), Ronald M. Green, *Religious Reason: The Rational and Moral Basis of Religious Belief* (New York: Oxford University Press, 1978), Paul Helm, ed., *Divine Commands and Morality* (New York: Oxford University Press, 1981), C. S. Lewis, *Mere Christianity* (New York: Macmillan, 1943), Immanuel Kant, *Critique of Practical Reason* (trans. by Lewis White Beck; New York: Liberal Arts Press, 1956), Basil Mitchell, *Morality: Religious and Secular* (Oxford: Clarendon, 1980), and H. P. Owen, *The Moral Argument for Christian Theism* (London: Allen & Unwin, 1965).

54. I. Kant, *Critique of Practical Reason*, 166.

55. See *Republic* 6, 507b.

56. For a critique of relativism, see J. Finnis, *Natural Law and Natural Rights* (Oxford: Oxford University Press, 1980), Norman Geisler, *Options in Contemporary Christian Ethics* (Grand Rapids: Baker, 1981), C. S. Lewis, *Miracles* (New York: Macmillan, 1947), Erwin Lutzer, *The Necessity of Ethical Absolutes* (Grand Rapids: Zondervan, 1981), and Roger Trigg, *Reason and Commitment* (London: Cambridge University Press, 1973).

57. C. S. Lewis, "The Case for Christianity," *The Best of C. S. Lewis* (New York: Iversen, 1969), 409.

58. Henry M. Morris, *Many Infallible Proofs* (San Diego: Creation Life, 1974), 117.

59. C. S. Evans, op. cit.,45.

60. "Wittgenstein's Lectures on Ethics," *Philosophical Review*, 1965, 47:7.

61. Hasting Rashdall, *The Theory of Good and Evil* (Oxford: Clarendon, 1907), 212.

62. Paul Kurtz, *Forbidden Fruit* (Buffalo, N.Y.: Prometheus, 1988), 65.

63. Richard Taylor, *Ethics, Faith, and Reason* (Englewood Cliffs, N.J.: Prentice Hall, 1985), 2–3.

64. D. M. Baillie, *Faith in God and Its Christian Consummation* (Edinburgh: T. & T. Clark, 1927), 173.

65. Jean-Paul Sartre, "Existentialism," *Existentialism and Human Emotions* (trans. Bernard Frechtman; New York: Philosophical Library, 1957), 22.

66. D. Elton Trueblood, *Philosophy of Religion* (New York: Harper & Brothers, 1957), 115.

67. Peter Berger, *A Rumor of Angels: Modern Society and the Rediscovery of the Supernatural* (Garden City, N.Y.: Doubleday, 1969), 52.

68. John Polkinghorne, *The Way the World Is* (London: SPCK, 1983), 33.

69. See Frank Morison, C. S. Lewis, Simon Greenleaf, Josh McDowell, and others.

70. Quoted in Frank Ballard, *The Miracles of Unbelief* (Edinburgh: Clark, 1913), 251.

71. Loraine Boettner, *Studies in Theology* (Philadelphia: Presbyterian & Reformed, 1970), 266.

72. Arnold Toynbee, *Civilization on Trial* (New York, Oxford University Press, 1948), 218.

73. H. G. Wells, *The Outline of History* (New York: Doubleday, 1971), 1.420.

74. C. S. Lewis, *Miracles* (New York: Macmillan, 1947), 113.

75. John W. Montgomery, *History and Christianity* (Downers Grove: InterVarsity, 1965), 58.

76. D. H. Van Daalen, *The Real Resurrection* (London: Collins, 1972), 41.

77. See Craig Blomberg, *The Historical Reliability of the Gospels* (Downers Grove: InterVarsity, 1987), Raymond E. Brown, *The Virginal Conception and Bodily Resurrection of Jesus* (New York: Paulist, 1973), William Craig, *The Son Rises* (Chicago: Moody, 1981), James D. G. Dunn, *The Evidence for Jesus* (Philadelphia: Westminster, 1985), R. T. France, *The Evidence for Jesus* (Downers Grove: InterVarsity, 1986), Joachim Jeremias, *New Testament Theology* (trans. John Bowden; New York: Scribner's & Macmillan, 1971), I. Howard Marshall, *I Believe in the Historical Jesus* (Grand Rapids: Eerdmans, 1977).

78. Quoted in G. A. Buttrick, ed., *The Interpreter's Dictionary of the Bible* (New York: [n.p.], 1962).

79. Yandall Woodfin, *With All Your Mind: A Christian Philosophy* (Nashville: Abingdon, 1980).

80. C. F. D. Moule, *The Phenomenon of the New Testament* (London: SCM, 1967), 13.

81. Quoted in Richard Riss, *The Evidence for the Resurrection of Jesus Christ*

(Minneapolis: Bethany Fellowship, 1977), 17.

82. Blaise Pascal, *Pensées No. 430* (trans. H. F. Stewart; New York: Random House, [n.d.]), [n.p.].

CHAPTER 2

1. J. Hick, *Christianity at the Centre*, 82.
2. Quoted in *Oliphant-Smith Debate* (Nashville: Gospel Advocate, 1929), 28.
3. Bertrand Russell, *Why I Am Not a Christian*, ed. Paul Edwards (London: George Allen and Unwin, 1957), 22.
4. Albert Camus, *The Myth of Sisyphus and Other Essays*, trans. Justin O'Brien (New York: Vintage, 1955), 40.
5. Albert Camus, *The Plague*, trans. Stuart Gilbert (New York: Modern Library, 1948), 196.
6. *Oliphant-Smith Debate*, 32.
7. D. E. Trueblood, *General Philosophy*, 226.
8. J. Edwin Orr, *The Faith That Persuades* (New York: Harper & Row, 1977), 80.
9. A. N. Whitehead, *Religion in the Making* (Cambridge: Cambridge University Press, 1936), 77.
10. John W. Wenham, "Response," in Geisler, *The Roots of Evil* (Grand Rapids: Zondervan, 1978), 89.
11. Hugh Silvester, *Arguing with God* (Downers Grove: InterVarsity, 1971), 36.
12. Quoted in Louis Cassels, *The Reality of God* (Scottdale, Penn.: Herald, 1972), 31.
13. R. C. Sproul, *Objections Answered* (Glendale, Calif.: G/L Pub., 1978), 131.
14. Brand Blanshard, *Reason and Belief* (London: [n.p.], 1962), 546.
15. Ed. L. Miller, *God and Reason: A Historical Approach to Philosophical Theology* (New York: Macmillan, 1972), 139.
16. David Hume, *Dialogues Concerning Natural Religion* (ed. Henry D. Aiken; New York: Hafner, 1948), p. 66.
17. For further insight see L. Russ Bush, *A Handbook for Christian Philosophy* (Grand Rapids: Zondervan, 1991).
18. *Compendium of Theology*, Chapter 141.
19. C. S. Lewis, *The Best of C. S. Lewis* (New York: Iversen, 1969), 429.
20. William Dyrness, *Christian Apologetics in a World Community* (Downers Grove: InterVarsity, 1983), 155.
21. Arlie J. Hoover, *Fallacies of Unbelief* (Abilene, Tex.: Biblical Research, 1975), 41.
22. Ibid.
23. Jean-Paul Sartre, *Existentialism and Humanism* (London: Methuen, 1948), 33.
24. Ibid., 30.
25. Quoted in *Christian Reflection* (ed. Walter Hooper; Grand Rapids: Eerdmans, 1967), 70.
26. D. H. Freeman, *A Philosophical Study of Religion*, 223.
27. Eric L. Mascall, *He Who Is*, 183.
28. C. S. Lewis, *Mere Christianity*, 429–430.
29. Richard L. Purtill, *Reason to Believe* (Grand Rapids: Eerdmans, 1974), 96.
30. C. E. M. Joad, *The Recovery of Belief* (London: Faber & Faber, 1952), 63.
31. E. L. Mascall, op. cit., 183.
32. Quoted in E. L. Mascall, 184.
33. Antony Flew, *God and Philosophy* (London: Hutchinson & Harcourt, 1966), 106.
34. Ed. L. Miller, op. cit., 143.
35. A. E. Wilder-Smith, *Why Does God Allow It?* (San Diego, Calif.: Master, 1980), 25–26.
36. Alvin Plantinga, *God, Freedom, and Evil* (Grand Rapids: Eerdmans, 1974), 10.
37. Mary Baker Eddy, *Science and Health with Key to the Scriptures* (Boston: The First Church of Christ, Scientist, 1994), 480.
38. Hamlet, Act ii, Scene ii, line 255, *Great Books of the Western World* Book 27 (Chicago: Encyclopaedia Britannica, 1952), 43.
39. Norman L. Geisler, *Philosophy of Religion*, 312.
40. Norman L. Geisler, *The Roots of Evil* (Grand Rapids: Zondervan, 1978), 18.
41. Norman L. Geisler, *Philosophy of Religion*, 312.
42. D. E. Trueblood, op. cit., 237.
43. W. Dyrness, op. cit., 156.
44. D. E. Trueblood, op. cit., 244.
45. J. O. Orr, op. cit., 81.
46. C. S. Lewis, *Mere Christianity*, 46–47.
47. Norman L. Geisler, *Philosophy of Religion*, 347.
48. E. J. Carnell, *An Introduction to Christian Apologetics* (Grand Rapids: Eerdmans, 1948), 302.
49. St. Augustine, *On Free Choice of the Will*, II, 18 (trans. Anna S. Benjamin and L. H. Hackstaff; Indianapolis, Ind.: Library of Liberal Arts, 1964).
50. C. S. Lewis, *The Problem of Pain*, 16.
51. Ed. L. Miller, op. cit., 144.
52. W. Dyrness, op. cit., 162.
53. John H. Gerstner, *Reasons For Faith* (Grand Rapids: Baker, 1967), 19.
54. John W. Montgomery, *The Suicide of*

Christian Theology (Minneapolis: Bethany Fellowship, 1975), 259.

55. V. A. Demant, *Difficulties* (London: Mowbray, 1958), 137.

56. C. S. Lewis, *The Problem of Pain*, 81.

57. G. K. Chesterton, *Orthodoxy* (Garden City, N.J.: Doubleday, 1959), 79.

58. Dorothy L. Sayers, *Christian Letters to a Post-Christian World* (Grand Rapids: Eerdmans, 1969), 14.

59. Quoted in N. L. Geisler, *Roots of Evil*, p. 90.

60. Quoted in Christopher E. Storrs, *Many Creeds: One Cross* (London: SCM, 1945), 80.

61. E. J. Carnell, *Christian Commitment: An Apologetic* (New York: Macmillan, 1957), 281.

62. Dorothy L. Sayers, *Creed or Chaos?* (New York: Harcourt, Brace and Company, 1949), 4.

CHAPTER 3

1. Patrick Masterson, *Atheism and Alienation* (Middlesex, England: Penguin, 1971), 13–14.

2. See E. Borne, *Atheism* (New York: Hawthorn, 1961), James Collins, *God in Modern Philosophy* (Chicago: Henry Regnery, 1959), Cornelio Fabro, *God in Exile* (New York: Newman, 1968) and R. C. Sproul, *The Psychology of Atheism* (Minneapolis: Bethany Fellowship, 1974).

3. Quoted in Alister McGrath, *Bridge-Building* (Leicester: InterVarsity, 1992), 116.

4. See Robert A. Morey, *The New Atheism and the Erosion of Freedom* (Minneapolis: Bethany House, 1986).

5. Paul Edwards, ed., *The Encyclopedia of Philosophy* (New York: Macmillan, 1972), 1.175.

6. Ludwig Feuerbach, *The Essence of Christianity* (New York: Harper Torchbooks, 1957), 226.

7. Michael Scriven, *Primary Philosophy* (New York: McGraw-Hill, 1966), 88.

8. D. E. Trueblood, *Philosophy of Religion*, 82.

9. Madalyn Murray O'Hair, *What on Earth is an Atheist?* (New York: Arno, 1972), 38.

10. Quoted in Vernon C. Grounds, *The Reason for Our Hope* (Chicago: Moody, 1945), 18.

11. Alan Richardson, ed., "Atheism," *A Dictionary of Christian Theology* (Philadelphia: Westminster, 1969), 18.

12. Harold O. J. Brown, "The Conservative Option," *Tension in Contemporary Theology* (ed. Stanley N. Gundry and Alan F. Johnson; Chicago: Moody, 1976), 334–35.

13. Colin Brown, *Philosophy and the Christian Faith*, 139.

14. Friedrich Nietzsche, *Thus Spoke Zarathustra* (New York: Random House, [n.d.]), 355.

15. L. Feuerbach, op. cit., 13.

16. Quoted in D. E. Trueblood, op. cit., 186.

17. Karl Marx and Friedrich Engels, *On Religion* (New York: Schocken, 1964), 41.

18. "Marx and Marxism" in *The New Encyclopaedia Britannica* (Chicago: Encyclopaedia Britannica, 1986), 23.573–74.

19. Karl Marx, *Economic and Philosophical Manuscripts* (1844) in Bottomore and Rubel, 85.

20. Colin Brown, op. cit., 142.

21. Ted Honderich, ed., *The Oxford Companion to Philosophy* (Oxford: Oxford University Press, 1995), 116.

22. B. Russell, *Why I Am Not a Christian*, 3–4.

23. Jean-Paul Sartre, *Being and Nothingness*, Part 4, Chapter 1.

24. Ronald Hepburn, in Antony Flew and Alasdair MacIntyre, *New Essays in Philosophical Theory* (New York: Macmillan, [n.d.]), 140.

25. Jean-Paul Sartre, *Words* (New York: George Braziller, 1964), 102.

26. For a good discussion on the subject see Terry Miethe & Antony Flew, *Does God Exist?* (San Francisco: Harper, 1991).

27. Antony G. N. Flew and Thomas B. Warren, *The Warren-Flew Debate* (Jonesboro, Ark.: National Christian, 1977), 240.

28. Ibid., 241.

29. Alvin Plantinga, *God and Other Minds*, 163.

30. J. L. Mackie, *The Miracle of Theism*.

31. L. Feuerbach, *The Essence of Christianity*.

32. Antony Flew, *God and Philosophy*.

33. Sigmund Freud, *The Future of an Illusion* (trans. by W. D. Robson-Scott; New York: Doubleday & Co., 1957).

34. W. Matson, *The Existence of God* (Ithaca, N.Y.: Cornell University Press, 1965).

35. B. Russell, *Why I Am Not a Christian*.

36. Walter Kaufmann, *Critique of Religion and Philosophy* (New York: Doubleday, 1961).

37. Colin Brown, *Miracles and the Critical Mind* (Grand Rapids: Eerdmans, 1984), J. Collins, *God in Modern Philosophy*, W. L.

Craig, *The Kalam Cosmological Argument*, W. L. Craig, *Knowing the Truth About the Resurrection* (Ann Arbor: Servant, 1988), Stephen T. Davis, *Logic and the Nature of God* (Grand Rapids: Eerdmans, 1983), Norman L. Geisler, *Miracles and Modern Thought* (Grand Rapids: Zondervan, 1982), Geisler and Corduan, *Philosophy of Religion*, Stanley L. Jaki, *The Origin of Science and the Science of Its Origin* (South Bend, Ind.: Regnery/Gateway, 1978), Terry L. Miethe, ed., *Did Jesus Rise From the Dead? The Resurrection Debate* (San Francisco: Harper & Row, 1987), Basil Mitchell, *Morality: Religious and Secular* (Oxford: Clarendon, 1980), J. P. Moreland, *Scaling the Secular City* (Grand Rapids: Baker, 1987), Thomas V. Morris, ed., *The Concept of God* (Oxford: Oxford University Press, 1987), Ronald H. Nash, *The Concept of God*, Ronald H. Nash, *Faith and Reason* (Grand Rapids: Zondervan, 1988), H. P. Owen, *The Moral Argument for Christian Theism*, A. Plantinga, *God, Freedom, and Evil*, Richard Swinburne, *The Coherence of Theism* (Oxford: Clarendon, 1977), *The Concept of Miracle* (New York: St. Martin's, 1970), *The Existence of God* (Oxford: Clarendon, 1979), F. R. Tennant, *Philosophical Theology* vol. 2 (Cambridge: Cambridge University Press, 1956), Charles B. Thaxton, Walter L. Bradley, and Roger L. Olsen, *The Mystery of Life's Origin: Reassessing Current Theories* (New York: Philosophical Library, 1984), K. E. Yandell, *Christianity and Philosophy*.

38. See R. L. Purtill, *Reason to Believe*, R. C. Sproul, *Psychology of Atheism*, and D. E. Trueblood, *Philosophy of Religion*.

39. See Gordon H. Clark, *The Philosophy of Science and Belief in God* (Nutley, N.J.: Craig Press, 1964), S. L. Jaki, *The Road of Science and the Ways to God*, and J. P. Moreland, *Scaling the Secular City*.

40. See G. K. Chesterton, *Orthodoxy* (London: Fontana, 1961) and Ronald H. Nash, *Christianity and the Hellenistic World* (Grand Rapids: Zondervan, 1984).

41. See J. Oliver Buswell, Jr., *A Systematic Theology of the Christian Religion* (Singapore: Christian Life Pub., 1994), W. L. Craig, *Reasonable Faith*, S. Hackett, *The Resurrection of Theism* (Grand Rapids: Baker, 1982) and M. Thompson, *A Modern Philosophy of Religion*.

42. Jules A. Baisnee, ed., *Readings in Natural Theology* (Westminster, Md.: Newman, 1962), 149.

43. This approach is challenged by philosophers such as Alvin Plantinga and Nicholas Wolterstorff in *Faith and Rationality: Reason and Belief in God* (London: University of Notre Dame Press, 1986).

44. See Antony Flew, *The Presumption of Atheism and Other Philosophical Essays on God, Freedom and Immortality* (New York: Barnes & Noble, 1976).

45. L. R. Bush, *A Handbook for Christian Philosophy*, 225.

46. William L. Craig, *The Existence of God and the Beginning of the Universe* (San Bernardino: Here's Life, 1979), 32.

47. J. P. Moreland, *Scaling the Secular City*, 92.

48. Ibid.

49. Bertrand Russell, *What I Believe* (New York: C. P. Dutton and Co., 1925), 13.

50. Friedrich Nietzsche, "The AntiChrist" in *The Portable Nietzsche* (trans. Walter Kaufmann; New York: The Viking Press, 1968), 627.

51. John Hick, *The Existence of God* (New York: Macmillan, 1964), 170–71.

52. J. A. Baisnee, op. cit., 149.

53. F. Nietzsche, *Thus Spoke Zarathustra*, 355.

54. Ernst L. Freud, ed., *Letters of Sigmund Freud* (London: Hogarth, 1961), 432.

55. F. Nietzsche, *The Portable Nietzsche* (ed. Walter Kaufmann; Princeton: Princeton University Press, 1968), 44.

56. A. Camus, *The Myth of Sisyphus*, 80.

57. Quoted in Mehto Ved, *Fly and the Fly-Bottle: Encounters with British Intellectuals* (Weidenfield & Nicolson, 1963), 41.

58. Francis Schaeffer, *The God Who is There* (Downers Grove: InterVarsity, 1968), 73–74.

59. Quoted in Leslie Badham, *Verdict on Jesus* (London: Hodder & Stoughton, 1950), 156.

60. Richard Coe, *Samuel Beckett* (New York: Grove, 1964), 18.

61. Bertrand Russell, *A Free Man's Worship* (Portland, Me.: Thomas Mosher, 1927), 6–7.

62. Robert J. Dean, *How Can We Believe?* (Nashville: Broadman, 1978), 25.

CHAPTER 4

1. Vernon C. Grounds, *The Reason For Our Hope*, 40.

2. Alan Hayward, *God Is* (Nashville: Thomas Nelson, 1978), 174–75.

3. J. H. Gerstner, *Reasons For Faith*, 80.

4. See R. Nash, *Christianity and the Hellenistic World*, Michael J. Wilkins and J. P. Moreland, *Jesus Under Fire* (Grand Rapids: Zondervan, 1995), C. Blomberg, *The Historical Reliability of the Gospels*, R. T. France, *The Evidence for Jesus* (Downers Grove: InterVarsity, 1986) and N. T. Wright, *Who Was Jesus?* (Grand Rapids: Eerdmans, 1992).

5. H. G. Wells, *The Outline of History*, 1.420.

6. Will Durant, "Caesar and Christ," in *The Story of Civilization* (New York: Simon & Schuster, 1944), 3.557.

7. Otto Betz, *What Do We Know About Jesus?* (London: SCM, 1968), 9.

8. F. F. Bruce, *The New Testament Documents* (London: InterVarsity, 1968), 119.

9. Jim McGuiggan, *If God Came* (Lubbock, Tex.: Montex, 1980), 33.

10. James Frazer, *The Golden Bough*, (London: Studley, 1951), 9.412.

11. Ibid.

12. Michael Green, *Runaway World* (London: InterVarsity, 1968), 2.

13. John Stuart Mill, *Essays on Nature, the Utility of Religion and Theism* (London: Longmans, 1874).

14. W. H. Fitchett, *The Beliefs of Unbelief* (London: Cassell, 1908), 178.

15. Herbert Butterfield, *Christianity and History* (London: George Bell & Sons, 1950), 129.

16. Frank Ballard, *Miracles*, 251.

17. F. F. Bruce, op. cit., 119.

18. Ibid., 114.

19. Ibid., 117.

20. Ibid., 118.

21. Flavius Josephus, *Antiquities of the Jews* ([n.n.], [n.p.], A.D. 93), XVIII.3.3.

22. Flavius Josephus, XX.9.1.

23. Ethelbert Stauffer, *Jesus and His Story* (New York: Alfred P. Knopf, 1959), 9.

24. M. Green, op. cit., 20.

25. F. F. Bruce, op. cit., 119.

26. C. S. Lewis, "What are We to Make of Jesus Christ?" in *God in the Dock: Essays on Theology and Ethics*, ed. Walter Hooper (Grand Rapids: Eerdmans, 1970), 157–58.

27. J. H. Gerstner, op. cit., 82.

28. Henry J. Heydt, *A Comparison of World Religions* (Fort Washington, Pa.: Christian Literature Crusade, 1967), 92–93.

29. J. O. Buswell, *A Systematic Theology of the Christian Religion* (Singapore: Christian Life Pub., 1994), 105.

30. John R. W. Stott, *Basic Christianity* (Chicago: InterVarsity, 1964), 26.

31. A. Hayward, op. cit., 175.

32. W. E. H. Lecky, *History of European Morals from Augustus to Charlemagne*, II (London: Longmans, Green, 1869), 88.

33. John Young, *The Case Against Christ* (London: Church Pastoral Aid Society, 1978), 83.

34. Quoted in F. Ballard, *Miracles*, 251.

35. J. H. Gerstner, op. cit., 81.

36. C. S. Lewis, *Mere Christianity*, 52–53.

37. C. H. Pinnock, *Reason Enough: A Case for the Christian Faith* (Downers Grove: InterVarsity, 1980), 90.

38. Richard L. Purtill, *Thinking About Religion* (Englewood Cliffs, N.J.: Prentice-Hall, 1978), 70.

39. Paul E. Little, *Know Why You Believe* (London: Scripture Union, 1968), 21.

40. James Edwin Orr, *The Resurrection of Jesus* (Joplin: College Press, 1972), 224.

41. B. B. Warfield, *The Person and Work of Christ* (Philadelphia: Puritan Reformed, 1950), 537.

42. R. Riss, *The Evidence for the Resurrection of Jesus Christ*, 104–105.

43. Thomas Arnold, *Sermons on the Christian Life: Its Hopes, Its Fears, and Its Close* (London: [n.p.], 1859), 324.

44. C. S. Lewis, *Miracles*, 306–307.

45. Philip Schaff, *The Person of Christ* (Boston: The American Tract Society, 1865), 5.

CHAPTER 5

1. George W. Dehoff, *Why We Believe the Bible* (Murfreesboro, Tenn.: Dehoff, 1974), 14.

2. Bernard Ramm, *Protestant Christian Evidences* (Chicago: Moody, 1953), 232–33.

3. Don Stewart, *You Be The Judge* (San Bernardino: Here's Life, 1983), 83.

4. Werner Keller, *The Bible as History* (trans. William Neil; New York: William Morrow, 1956), 45.

5. Carl Jung, *Modern Man In Search of a Soul* (trans. Dell and Bayress; New York: Harcourt Brace, 1933), 264.

6. R. C. Sproul, *Knowing Scripture* (Downers Grove: InterVarsity, 1978), 23.

7. L. Wittgenstein, *Tractatus Logico-Philosophicus*, 145, 147.

8. J. W. Montgomery, *The Suicide of Christian Theology*, 366.

9. R. C. Sproul, op. cit., 24.

10. Clark Pinnock, *Set Forth Your Case* (Chicago: Moody, 1971), 85.

24. S. M. Thompson, *A Modern Philosophy of Religion*, 237.

25. J. I. Packer, *Keep Yourself from Idols* (London: Church Book Room, 1964), 13.

26. C. E. M. Joad, *Return to Philosophy* (London: Faber & Faber, 1958), 35.

27. E. Stanley Jones, *The Victory Through Surrender* (Nashville: Abingdon, 1966), 27.

28. F. L. Woodward, *Some Sayings of Buddha* (Oxford), 283.

29. Paul Reps, *Zen Flesh, Zen Bones: A Collection of Zen and Pre-Zen Writings* (New York: Anchor, [n.d.]), 45.

30. D. T. Suzuki, op. cit., 19.

31. D. T. Suzuki, *An Introduction to Zen Buddhism* (New York: Grove, 1964), 41.

32. W. J. Petersen, *Those Curious New Cults*, 173.

33. Quoted in Daniel Cohen, *The New Believers: Young Religion in America* (New York: M. Evans & Co., 1975), 112.

34. Quoted in R. D. Clements, *God and the Gurus*, 27.

35. W. Cantwell Smith, *Question of Religious Truth* (New York: Scribners, 1967), p. 74.

36. *The Upanishads*, 30–31.

37. P. Reps, *Zen Flesh and Zen Bones*, 118.

38. Quoted in Swami Prabhavananda, *The Spiritual Heritage of India* (Hollywood: Vedanta, 1963), 45.

39. Quoted in Joseph Head and S. L. Cranston, eds., *Reincarnation: The Phoenix Fire Mystery* (New York: Warner, 1977), 61.

40. R. C. Sproul, *Knowing Scripture*, 17.

41. C. S. Lewis, *Miracles* (London: Fontana Books, 1960), 18.

42. Sproul, Gerstner, and Lindsley, *Classical Apologetics*, 76.

43. C. E. M. Joad, *The Book of Joad* (London: Faber & Faber, 1944), 72–73.

44. H. J. Paton, *The Modern Predicament* (London: Macmillan, 1955), 58.

45. O. Guinness, op. cit., 210.

46. Alan Watts, *The Spirit of Zen* (New York: Grove, 1958), 80.

47. Sohaku Ogata, *Zen for the West* (New York: Dial, 1959), 17–19.

48. *The Upanishads*, Mand. 7.

49. Clark H. Pinnock, *Set Forth Your Case* (Nutley, N.J.: Craig, 1967), 46.

50. C. E. M. Joad, *The Recovery of Belief*, 98.

51. Paul T. Arveson, "Dialogic – A Systems Approach to Understanding," *Journal of American Scientific Affiliation*, June 1978, 51.

52. C. S. Lewis, *Miracles* (New York: Macmillan, 1948), 11.

53. Walter Pahnke, *LSD, Man and Society* (eds. Richard DeBold and Russell Leaf; London: Faber & Faber, 1969), 70.

54. C. G. Jung, foreword to *An Introduction to Zen Buddhism*, by Suzuki, 15.

55. W. J. Petersen, op. cit., 172.

56. R. E. L. Masters and Jean Houston, *Varieties of Psychedelic Experience* (London: Turnstone, 1966), 252.

57. Quoted in Colin Weightman and Robert W. McCarthy, *A Mirage from the East* (Adelaide, Australia: Lutheran, 1977), 8.

58. B. B. Warfield, *Biblical and Theological Studies* (Philadelphia: Presbyterian & Reformed, 1952), 455.

59. David Hugh Freeman, *Know Your Self* (Nutley, N.J.: Craig, 1976), 79.

60. W. J. Petersen, op. cit., 172.

CHAPTER 8

1. *Time*, April 16, 1979, 40, 49.

2. Bruce Demarest, *General Revelation* (Grand Rapids: Zondervan, 1982), 17.

3. Don McCurry, "Why Are Muslims So Militant?" *Christianity Today*, March 1980, 27.

4. Frithjof Schuon, *Understanding Islam* (trans. D. M. Matheson; Baltimore, Md.: Penguin, 1972), 56.

5. J. N. D. Anderson, ed., *The World's Religions* (London: InterVarsity, 1975), 120.

6. Maurice Bucaille, *The Bible, The Quran and Science* (Paris: North American Trust, 1978), 127.

7. Maulvi Muhammad Ali, *Muhammad and Christ* (Lahore: Ahmadiah Anjuman-i-Ishaet-l-Islam, 1921), 15.

8. M. M. Bucaille, op. cit., 108.

9. F. F. Bruce, *The New Testament Documents: Are They Reliable?* (Grand Rapids: Eerdmans, 1977), 15.

10. J. Jeremias, *New Testament Theology, The Proclamation of Jesus* (New York: Scribner's, 1971), 37.

11. Clark Pinnock, *Set Forth Your Case* (Nutley, N.J.: Craig, 1967), 52.

12. S. E. Frost, *The Sacred Writings of the World's Great Religions* (Philadelphia: Blakiston, 1948), 67.

13. McDowell and Gilchrist, *The Islam Debate*, 50.

14. L. Bevan Jones, *The People of the Mosque* (Calcutta: YMCA, 1939), 277.

15. D. Freeman, *A Philosophical Study of Religion*, 122–23.

16. William McElwee Miller, "Islam," *Religions*

in a Changing World (ed. Howard F. Vos; Chicago: Moody, 1959), 70.

17. Ibid.

18. Thomas Hughes, *Dictionary of Islam* (Clifton, N.J.: Reference, 1965), 53.

19. Phil Parshall, *New Paths in Muslim Evangelism: Evangelical Approaches to Contextualization* (Grand Rapids: Baker, 1980), 142.

20. Robert Brow, *Religion, Origins and Ideas* (London: Tyndale, 1966), 89–90.

21. P. Parshall, op. cit., 143.

22. Dale Rhoton, *The Logic of Faith* (Bromley, Kent: STL, 1972), 74.

23. J. S. Wright, "The Perspicuity of Scripture," *Theological Student's Fellowship Bulletin*, Summer 1959, 7.

24. J. W. Montgomery, *How Do We Know There is a God?*, 14.

25. Abdullah Yusuf Ali, *The Holy Quran: Text, Translation and Commentary* (Qatar National Printing Press, 1946), 230.

26. Maulvi Muhammad Ali, op. cit., 158–59.

27. J. W. Montgomery, *History and Christianity,* 77.

28. Quoted in Irwin H. Linton, *A Lawyer Examines the Bible* (Grand Rapids: Baker, 1943), 11.

29. Quoted in Wilbur M. Smith, *Therefore Stand* (New Caanan, Conn.: Keats Pub., 1981), 425.

30. F. Morison, *Who Moved the Stone?*

31. Quoted in Dale Rhoton, op. cit., 90.

RECOMMENDED READING

Chapter 1

Farrer, Austin. *Finite and the Infinite*. New York: Seabury, 1979.

Hick, John, ed. *Arguments for the Existence of God*. New York: Herder, 1971.

Mascall, Eric. *He Who Is*. New York: Longmans, Green, 1943.

Mavrodes, George, ed. *The Rationality of Belief in God*. Englewood Cliffs: Prentice-Hall, 1970.

Reichenbach, Bruce. *The Cosmological Argument: A Reassessment*. Springfield: Charles C. Thomas, 1972.

Sillem, Edward. *Ways of Thinking About God*. London: Darton, Longman & Todd, 1961.

Swinburne, Richard. *The Existence of God*. Oxford: Clarendon, 1979.

Chapter 2

Geisler, Norman L. *Roots of Evil*. Grand Rapids: Zondervan, 1978.

Hick, John. *Evil and the God of Love*. New York: Macmillan, 1966.

Lewis, C. S. *The Problem of Pain*. New York: Macmillan, 1948.

Pike, Nelson, ed. *God and Evil*. Englewood Cliffs, N.J.: Prentice Hall, 1964.

Plantinga, Alvin. *God, Freedom, and Evil*. Grand Rapids: Eerdmans, 1974.

Wenham, John W. *The Goodness of God*. Downers Grove: InterVarsity, 1974.

Chapter 3

Borne, Etienne. *Atheism*. New York: Hawthorn, 1961.

Collins, James. *God in Modern Philosophy*. Chicago: Henry Regnery, 1959.

Grisez, Germain. *Beyond the New Theism*. South Bend, Ind.: University of Notre Dame Press, 1975.

Lepp, Ignace. *Atheism in Our Time*. New York: Macmillan, 1964.

Schilling, S. Paul. *God in an Age of Atheism*. Nashville: Abingdon, 1969.

Sproul, R. C. *The Psychology of Atheism*. Minneapolis: Bethany House Fellowship, 1974.

Strunk, Orlo, Jr. *The Choice Called Atheism*. Nashville: Abingdon, 1969.

Chapter 4

Anderson, J. N. D. *Christianity: The Witness of History*. London: Tyndale, 1969.

France, R. T. *The Evidence for Jesus*. Downers Grove: InterVarsity, 1976.

Marshall, I. Howard. *I Believe in the Historical Jesus*. Grand Rapids: Eerdmans, 1977.

Mitton, C. Leslie. *Jesus: The Fact Behind the Faith*. Grand Rapids: Eerdmans, 1977.

Morison, Frank. *Who Moved the Stone?* New York: Barnes & Noble, 1962.

Moule, C. F. D. *The Birth of the New Testament*. San Francisco: Harper & Row, 1981.

Wright, Tom. *Jesus and the Victory of God*. London: SPCK, 1993.

Chapter 5

Bruce, F. F. *The New Testament Documents: Are they Reliable?* Grand Rapids: Eerdmans, 1956.

Clark, Gordon H. *God's Hammer: The Bible and its Critics*. Jefferson: The Trinity Foundation, 1982.

Radmacher, Earl D., ed. *Can We Trust the Bible?* Wheaton: Tyndale, 1979.

Robinson, John A. T. *Can We Trust the New Testament?* Grand Rapids: Eerdmans, 1977.

Staudinger, Hugo. *The Trustworthiness of the Gospels*. Edinburgh: Handsel, 1981.

Warfield, B. B. *The Inspiration and Authority of the Bible*. Philadelphia: Presbyterian & Reformed, 1958.

Wenham, John W. *Christ and the Bible*. Downers Grove: InterVarsity, 1973.

Chapter 6

Anderson, J. N. D., ed. *The World's Religions.* Grand Rapids: Eerdmans, 1976.

Bavinck, J. H. *The Church Between Temple and Mosque.* Grand Rapids: Eerdmans, 1981.

Fernando, Ajith. *The Christian's Attitude Toward World Religions.* Wheaton: Tyndale, 1978.

Hesselgrave, David J. *Communicating Christ Cross-Culturally.* Grand Rapids: Zondervan, 1978.

Hume, Robert E. *The World's Living Religions.* New York: Scribner's, 1929.

Neill, Stephen. *Crises of Belief.* London: Hodder & Stoughton, 1984.

Newbigin, Lesslie. *The Finality of Christ.* Richmond: John Knox, 1969.

Chapter 7

Chang, Lit-Sen. *Zen-Existentialism.* Philadelphia: Presbyterian and Reformed, 1969.

Clark, David K. *The Pantheism of Alan Watts.* Downers Grove: InterVarsity, 1978.

Hackett, Stuart C. *Oriental Philosophy: A Westerner's Guide to Eastern Thought.* Madison: University of Wisconsin Press, 1979.

Hunt, John. *Pantheism and Christianity.* New York: Kennikat, 1970.

Means, Pat. *The Mystical Maze.* Campus Crusade for Christ, 1976.

Zaehner, R. C. *Mysticism, Sacred and Profane.* Oxford: Clarendon, Oxford Paperbacks, 1961.

Chapter 8

Cragg, Kenneth. *The Call of the Minaret.* New York: Oxford University Press, 1956.

Deshmukh, I. O. *The Gospel and Islam.* Bombay: Gospel Literature Service, 1982.

Marrison, G. E. *The Christian Approach to the Muslim.* London: Edinburgh House, 1959.

McDowell, Josh and John Gilchrist. *The Islam Debate.* San Bernardino: Here's Life, 1983.

Miller, William McElwee. *A Christian's Response to Islam.* Philadelphia: Presbyterian & Reformed, 1976.

Pfander, C. G., *The Mizan-Ul-Haqq (Balance of Truth).* Revised by W. St. Clair Tisdall. London: The Religious Tract Society, 1910.

Tisdall, W. St. Clair. *Christian Reply to Muslim Objections.* Villach, Austria: Light of Life, 1980.